Social Media Marketing Plan How To

Build A Magnetic Brand Making You A Known Influencer. Go from Zero to One Million Followers In 30 Days. Apply The 1-Page Advertising Secret to Stand Out

Gary Murphy

Legal Notice

This book is copyright protected. This book is only for personal use. You cannot amend, distribute, sell, use, quote or paraphrase any part, or the content within this book, without the consent of the author or publisher.

Disclaimer Notice:

Please note the information contained within this document is for educational and entertainment purposes only. All effort has been executed to present accurate, up to date, and reliable, complete information. No warranties of any kind are declared or implied. Readers acknowledge that the author is not engaging in the rendering of legal, financial, medical or professional advice. The content within this book has been derived from various sources. Please consult a licensed professional before attempting any techniques outlined in this book.

By reading this document, the reader agrees that under no circumstances is the author responsible for any losses, direct or indirect, which are incurred as a result of the use of information contained within this document, including, but not limited to, — errors, omissions, or inaccuracies.

Contents

Chapter 1:
What Is A Brand

The Brand

A brand is what makes a person or business stand out from others. It is the way the target audience perceives a product, service, or experience due to its design, logo, name, and slogans.

The Business

A business is an organization which tries to satisfy the needs of various individuals to gain profits by selling products and services that solve the problem of the audience.

What Differentiates A Brand from A Business?

A business focuses more on how to generate profits by offering products and services to its target audience. The brand, on the other hand, is a culmination of the experience that members of the target audience will have any time they interact with the business.

Elements of A Brand

Various elements make a brand. Understanding these elements is a more straightforward way to understand a brand better. These include brand identity, compass, personality, voice, and more.

Brand Compass

The basic facts about a brand are summarized within the brand compass. It includes the strategic objectives, mission, purpose, values, and vision of a brand. The brand compass is the result of the research, positioning, and brand strategy.

Brand Personality

The emotional and behavioral qualities of a brand form the brand personality. These are traits which closely relate with the brand. Through the brand personality, it is possible to connect with the target audience. A brand identity makes a brand easy to identify by individuals loyal to the brand. There are some aspects of a brand which also form the brand personality. These include the brand logo, its design, tagline, and more.

Brand Name and Tagline

The brand name is one of the easiest ways through which your audience can interact with the brand. It also applies to the tagline. Coming up with a tagline and a brand name requires testing, brainstorming, market research, and refinement. Through these processes, the brand name and slogan will be unique and meaningful. The values of a brand are usually identifiable from the name and tagline. It also differentiates a brand from its competition.

Brand Image

A brand image is merely the expectations that the target audience has a brand. It through the brand image that the target audience can predict the next step a brand will take. Through the brand image Apple has developed, none of their customers will be expecting an iPhone with running on the Android operating system. Also, it is also possible to predict that the net iPhone will run on iOS with improvements to the features which the phone offers. It is a clear indication of the brand image which the company has developed.

Brand Identity

There are a few things which are present in a brand strategy. These will include the promise, purpose, and personality of a brand. The brand identity is a visual representation of all these aspects. It is the real meaning behind the brand logo. As a visual, it should be able to communicate the core ideas of the brand to anyone who sees it. It is also straightforward to promote easy identification. Combining the logo with a tagline is a method which creates a brand identity that is recognizable worldwide.

Brand Voice and Messaging

The brand voice and its messaging determine how the brand will engage with its audience. These two elements are essential in delivering the personality, purpose, and promise of a brand. It also instills humanity in the brand. The brand voice should be easily recognizable by your audience. It doesn't matter the channel through which the message is coming.

Brand Website

The brand website is where your brand delivers content to engage with its audience. Using smartphones, your audience can access the brand website on the go and in any location. Providing a high-quality brand experience is more cost-effective through the brand website.

Brand Equity

The value of a brand is what I refer to as brand equity. It includes both the tangible and intangible aspects such as revenue, strategic benefits, and market shares.

Brand Gap

The disparity between what a brand can do and the promises the brand makes form the brand gap. For a brand to be successful, it needs a low brand gap. It implies that the brand should be able to deliver on the promises it makes to its customers. Promising a superior quality product at a low price and delivering an inferior quality product at a low price will cause a considerable brand gap.

Why Invest in Branding?

The perception of a business often determines if it will invest in a brand or not. The main reason for this difference in perception is the inability to relate a brand to the increase in returns directly. In truth, there is no way to evaluate the value of a brand. It is why a lot of businesses hesitate. If you cannot assess the value, why do you need to build a brand? A lot of businesses consider a brand to be an investment. As such, it is just an additional expense. Realizing that a brand is the only way to influence the behavior of the target customer will change this belief. Incorporating a brand into the long-term strategy of the business will yield profits all through the life of the company. Here are some of the benefits of a brand:

Branding Improves Recognition

An essential element of a brand is the brand logo. The logo serves as the face of the business. It is the first thing your audience will recollect about your brand. To design a logo, having a professional design is your best bet. The logo needs to be simple and easy to remember. A logo should reflect your ideal company image to your audience. If your company is within a niche in the gaming industry, having a gamepad on a stack of books can be misleading to your audience. Your target audience needs to be able to tell what your company does by a simple look at its logo.

Branding Creates Trust

By creating a brand, it is possible to develop trust between the company and its customers. A great brand will also provide the look of an industry expert. The target audience is usually willing to interact with a brand since it offers a professional outlook. It is noticeable in the way it provides its services and performs its operations.

Branding Promotes Marketing

A brand is the most effective form of marketing a business can invest in. If a brand is recognized, it becomes easier for marketing to achieve its goals. Since developing a brand will require a lot of market research, it is possible to use this market research to reach the target audience.

Branding Builds Financial Value

Building a strong brand usually increases the value of a business. It is the main reason why a company will have valuable stocks. The stocks don't indicate the actual value of the assets but the value of the brand. A company that grows its brand properly will reap its benefits during IPO sales or when it needs to source for funds. In addition to the increase in share prices, your customers will also be able to justify the rise in the prices of products. It becomes the ideal definition of customers buying a brand. An established brand name makes it easy to attract premium prices. The increase in value through a brand also makes it profitable for a business owner any time the need to sell the business arises.

Motivation to You and Your Employees

The brand is something that you are working towards. It is essential to have something to work towards to serve as a goal. That is what your brand is to your employees. A strong brand will cause employees to feel a sense of pride when working. The brand is something the entire team can rally around.

Branding Generates New Customers

Having a strong brand develops customer loyalty. Word-of-mouth marketing is one of the benefits of having loyal customers. It is also well-known that customer loyalty is an essential factor in business. Since your loyal customers will be assisting in the marketing of your brand, you are more likely to attract your ideal customers. These are customers who will also be willing to buy into your brand and remain loyal to the brand.

It Allows You Charge A Premium Price

According to the old saying, people buy brands and not products. For these reasons, individuals don't mind paying premium prices for pre-mium brands. Branding offers you the chance to place yourself as a leader in the industry with a persuasive set of values none of your competitors offer. Brands that make themselves unique can validate their worth and charge higher than their competitors for their ser-vices and products. As we are all aware, increase in price means an increase in revenue.

Close Sales with More Ease

The difference between trying to sell a brand that outdated and bor-ing, and one that is fresh and unique is like the difference between our former landlines and the new android phone. It is easier to sell a properly defined brand because they have established their position in the narrative of their brand. The arguments as to how your brand as unique and superior services or products has already being portrayed through the strategy of your brand. With a compelling and cohesive brand, most of the salesperson's work has already been done before the first conversation. Branding offers your sales team the upper hand it requires to swiftly, easily and confidently close deals.

Minimize Cost of Marketing

A brand which is well-articulated and cohesive enhances the effectiveness and efficiency of your marketing initiatives. By understanding your audience better alongside customer interviews, you will be able to create campaigns with a very significant message which targets your most relevant customer groups. You won't have to waste any more efforts on blind messaging. Brand cohesiveness also implies that any effort you make is incorporated with ease as all your initiatives aid in reinforcing one another. Your bold identity also implies that you differentiate your campaigns right from the start. Lastly, the templates and guidelines that come up from the process of branding make certain that you do not have to revamp the wheel on design each time you want to create another marketing initiative.

Tips to Take Control of Your Business Brand Identity

Establish your visual identity which goes with your projects and vision, or the target audience your organization wishes to work with

Pay attention to your reputation online, so you don't get surprised. Ask satisfied clients to offer you great reviews on Google or other review sites which help in catering to your market niche

Provide the experience your customers expect from all interaction that takes place from phone conversations, customer service, websites and sent emails. Treat your clients the way you would want a company to treat you if you were a client

Broaden your visibility on social networks and your community. Developing relationships are essential to building a brand, and the best method of doing it is to aid individuals in ways that make you stand out.

Do not forget that if you own a business, you have a brand. It is up to you to decide what to do with it and determine how others perceive you. If your brand goes with your visions and places emphasis on the requirements of your target audience, it can aid in attracting the appropriate customers to your organization.

Brand Evaluation

It is any meaningful and relevant feedback regarding the brand. Is the brand reaching its target audience? The feedback should come from the target audience for it to be relevant. If the feedback on a brand is coming from family and friends, it may not mirror the actual problems of the brand. There are specific indications that a brand is not doing too well.

"What Is A Brand?"

This is a problem that is common to a lot of businesses. Many businesses do not recognize a brand or its importance. Some businesses may also neglect the brand for a few years. It doesn't matter how important the business is to you as an entrepreneur; the brand is also a part of the business. Creating a brand platform makes it easy for your team to begin building.

There Is Nothing Unique About the Brand

No brand is built as an exact copy of a more successful brand. Nonetheless, there are often subtle similarities between certain brands. When evaluating the uniqueness of a brand, it is essential to ask a few questions. Questions like how often do competitors think up an event like what you had in mind? Are my competitors usually making comments like what you will make as a brand? These can be simple pointers to a lack of uniqueness in your brand. If you can state multiple areas where your brand differs from the competition, then this is not an issue. A competitor continually coming up with your ideas signifies the need for re-evaluation.

People Misunderstand the Brand

The goal of a brand is to connect with its target audience. It is evident that the target audience should have a clear understanding of what the brand offers. If there is a clear understanding of a brand by its target audience, other audiences should also be able to understand that it is not their ideal brand. It is crucial since you don't want to build a following or email list full of people who are irrelevant to the brand. It will usually lead to a waste of resources. The wrong audience will also misunderstand the brand message making it meaningless. Can people easily recollect what the brand does? Is it easy to describe?

Drop-In Conversions

A drop-in conversion rates over a period is an issue you need to look out for. As soon as a brand notices this trend, it is time to identify the cause. It could be an issue with the perception of the brand. Changes in this perception may also be a cause. It could also indicate a problem with the marketing strategy of the brand. It is a clear case of a branding strategy that doesn't effectively communicate the brand to the target audience. The numbers will only show that there is a problem. It is only through brand evaluation that the brand can identify the problem.

Chapter 2:
Social Media and Personal Branding

A lot of people have defined social media as applications that have been installed on their phones or tablets, but the plain fact is that social media started as a tool used for communication on computers. Social media can be defined as websites and application that are initially designed for people to have easy access to information which they could also in turn share efficiently to one another within a given period. The misconception that social media is an app that is meant for phones, smartphones to be precise, arise from the fact that most users of social media make use of apps to have access to the various tools that they want to make use of.

In truth, the ability to have easy access to photos, events, opinions of others and other information generally within a short period has done a lot of good. It has helped to change the way people live their lives, and it has also contributed one way or the other to improve the businesses of people, the way to run their business to be precise. Retail traders that engage the services of social media as an essential part of their marketing strategy always get impressive results. We also know that the best way to successfully engage social media is to treat it equally without any extra attachment as the other forms of marketing are also addressed.

The History of Social Media

The development of social media started many years ago, evidence of which is seen in some sites of today such as Facebook. The roots of social media are quite deeper than anybody can ever imagine.

Before The 1900s

Letters were the earliest means of communication. It is a means that was used to communicate across long distances, and it is delivered through passing from one hand to the other. Postal services were developed as far back as 550 B.C. Though it may be considered primitive, this delivery system is on the verge of spreading wide even in centuries to come.

Another means of communication known as telegraph was introduced in the year 1792. This medium enabled the delivery of long-distance messages. It is a medium that is so fast that it was quicker than sending a horse rider to deliver. The only thing about this form of communication is that the information it could carry is usually short. The method was anyway a new revolutionary means for sending messages or information across to people. The technique is no longer common outside the banking sector, but it still made delivery of letters easy in the year 1855 through a pneumatic post. It transported capsules from one location to the other using pressurized air tubes.

The telephone was created in the year 1890 and a year later, which is 1891, radio signals were also produced. In the 1800s, there were two significant discoveries in the last decade. Though modernized versions have taken over their predecessors, these forms of technology are still in use. These methods, telephone line, and radio signals have helped people over the years to communicate at high speed to people in faraway places at a given time. These inventions are like a new experience for the whole of humanity.

Development of Social Media in the 20th Century

In the 20th century, technology took a new turn as changes were occurring rapidly. The invention of the first ever supercomputers was in the 1940s, and after that, engineers and scientists began to brainstorm on different ways to connect these computers in such a way that network is created between them. This new development led to the discovery of the Internet. The development of the early versions of the internet like CompuServe started in the 1960s. Baby steps were also taken towards emailing at this period. As at the 70s, there had been significant improvements in networking technology, and virtual newsletters were available as a means of communication among users of UseNet. It was created in 1979.

In the 1980s, the transition of computers into household items had begun as home computers were being installed in homes. Social media was also becoming more stylish. In 1988, IRCs were used for the first time, and its popularity grew well into the 1990s. Six degrees was the first social media site to be recognized, and it was created in 1979. Users had the opportunity to create a profile and meet friends on Six Degrees. The original blogs also became popular in the year 1999, and it did a job of creating a social media stir that is still popular until today.

The Present Day

The popularity of social media began to grow immensely with the aid of the invention of blogging sites. Sites such as Myspace and LinkedIn became prominent sites in the early 2000s, sites such as photo bucket and Flicker aided online photo sharing. The creation of YouTube in 2005 gave people a new experience. A unique experience that enabled people to communicate and share the news in both far and near places. Facebook and Twitter also became available to people for use all over the world, and these sites still retain their status on the internet as the most popular sites. Some other sites such as Tumblr, Spotify, Foursquare and Pinterest were also created to fill up specific spaces in social networking.

In recent times, so many social networking sites have been created such that they are now interlinked to one another. The result of this is that users can now reach as many people as possible or even as many as they want without having to breach the one-to-one relationship they are privileged within communication. The future of social media in decades and even centuries to come is quite not clear as speculations can only be made. The only clear fact about it is that it will always exist in one way or the other if human living is concerned.

Your Personal Branding

Your personal branding has to do with the way you package yourself. It is the combination of the unique way you do the things that you want the world to see about you, a combination of your skills, experience, personality such that it tells your story, portrays the way you comport yourself, shows your behavior, spoken words, written words, and attitudes. Your personal branding is what people use to judge your professional state. Your personal brand could be a combination of how people look at you in real life, the kind of things the media says about you, the type of impression that forms in people's mind from the information they can get about you from social media.

You can choose to ignore your personal brand to enable it to grow naturally. By this, your personal brand tends to be disorganized and beyond your control. You can also choose to form your personal brand into what it is that you want it to be. Before the invention of the Internet, your business card was the only personal brand you have. The only people who were heard of by everyone or most people were those that have high profiles in the media, those who are referred to as hot cakes, also those who appeared as the face of advertisements. But in the world of today where there is no discreteness in social media; every piece of information is spilled, and there is a lower tendency for anonymity.

Why You Would Want A Personal Brand

Your personal brand can be a significant factor. It can be of crucial importance to your profession. It has to do with your presentation before potential and already made clients. It enables you to ensure that you are presented to people in the exact form which you want not in some other and probably detrimental way. It helps you to be able to know your strengths, your weaknesses, and your passions as well. It presents a kind of make-believe image that makes people believe they know you more than they do. It helps people to have a higher trust in you because they feel they know you; this applies to even public figures which they have never met personally. Clear evidence of this is noticeable during the period of election. A lot of people do not take their time to do their findings on the views of the candidates on issues that matter to them; they go directly for a recognized person. It should not come as a surprise that candidates with strong personalities irrespective of their political orientation succeed in politics. It cannot be argued for instance that Donald Trump has built a strong personal brand that helped a lot of people trustingly cast their votes in his favor.

The Importance of Social Media in Personal Branding

To be influential in today's world, you need to create a solid personal brand. Having a personal brand is important because it makes you different from every other person in your field. Your personal brand can help you show off your knowledge and skills in that area. It gives people something to remember you for and separates you from the multitudes surrounding you.

Modern people dislike advertising on a general level; neither do they trust the brands that make them. However, they like and trust people that they feel they know. This observation has influenced how businesses think to market themselves and has led to the popularity and general success of influence marketing today.

Personalizing the main people in a business is now a trend. But while this is easy for small businesses run by sole proprietors, it is difficult for larger companies. Some of them have mastered it well though.

It is logical that before trying to sell a company's message, the owner or manager should first establish a relationship with the potential market. Observe the following on how social media improves personal branding:

Social Media Helps You Announce to The World What You Have to Offer

By function and features, you should note that social media helps you spread the word out about your business. As a result, by not being actively involved in social media, you are significantly limiting your business' chance of getting a good exposure.

Through social media, you can gain brand recognition, develop the brand, and build a likeness for it. On social media, you can create a loyal customer or fan base. More importantly, you can develop your relationship with your target market.

People you engage with on social media including followers and fans will do business with you and refer their friends within and outside social media to you for future business.

Social Media Helps to Enhance Your Search Engine Visibility

Search engine optimization (SEO) works in increasing visibility of contents in search engine results. Many factors influence the search engine ranking of your website and having a social media presence is one of them. Other important factors include mobile optimization of your site, page load speed, linking relationships, and web content. You will have more visibility due to a higher rank in the search engine. Rankings of 95% and usually land on the first page of the search result.

You can maintain a constant social media presence when you always post good content that resonates with your audience. Doing this will have a positive impact on your search results and create more linking relationships. In short, you can't ignore social media if you want high visibility for your business.

Social Media Helps You See into The World of Potential Customers

In every business and every industry, knowing about your potential market is a big priority. Without knowing your audience and understanding what resonates with them, you can't create and deliver the kind of content that they need to see to be willing to patronize your business.

You have the option of conducting research through focus groups and administering surveys, but these can be costly, frivolous, and ineffective in the long run because they can't be done frequently enough.

On the other hand, you can take advantage of social media which encourages interaction on mutual grounds and exchange of information. You get to learn more about your market while they can also explore your social media pages to learn more about you.

No doubt, when used properly, social media is a cheap, fast, and effective way to get information about your audience. You can use that information to grow your business.

Social Media Can Increase Your Web Traffic

Social media is an excellent way for you to be found online and another avenue to invite people to your website. Your every activity on social media is a potential way to lead people to your business website. Therefore, the more you engage your social media pages and your followers, the higher the chances you have at bringing traffic to patronize your site.

The way this works is that your social media will raise curiosity about and your business and in trying to find out more, your audience will do find their way into your website. Social media gives a good return on engagement and will be worth the time you invest in it towards your business. You can create the kind of image about you that you want your audience to see.

Social Media Is Very Popular in The New Age

It is common knowledge to even non-tech readers or fans and marketing novices that social media is very popular among customers of businesses and products.

Recent research at Pew Research center shows that 65 percent of American adults are active users of social media networks. What this implies is that almost every customer that visits you is a social media user.

The Facebook network currently has a record of 1.7 billion active users in a month. For small businesses, this is easily an excellent place to start getting involved with social media marketing.

Facebook is developed in such a way that there is hardly a business that will not benefit from establishing and managing a presence there. It is very dynamic in function, user-friendly, and provides a broad and extensive audience, considering the massive number of users. Facebook is such a friendly place to start that extending from there to other social media networks will be very easy for you.

Social Media Is More Budget Friendly

Most big social media networks offer advertising packages that are easy on the budget. As a small business owner, you can take advantage of this to reach your audience and provide them with your content. These services are a good bargain for the low prices because social media networks now filter what gets to each user's feeds and your generic content may be drowned in the mix.

Traditional advertising costs more than social media methods, so this is good news since you no longer must break the bank to reach out to the public, grow your audience, and increase your business.

Social Media Encourages Two-Way Communication

On social media, you can receive feedback from your audience and learn about their interests and preferences.

You can get to know your customers better by asking questions that encourage them to share their thoughts and ideas with you. On your part, you can also give them quick responses without going through the hassles of using the phone or thinking about whether they will get your answers or not.

Social Media Users Are Consistent

One interesting thing to note about people who use social media is that they mean it in every single essence when they say they use social media. Reliable statistics have shown that in the USA alone, the average social media user checks his account 17 times in a day to catch up on news feeds.

It implies that they are more likely to receive your social media contents several times in a day and be updated on your business, even while they hardly pay any visits to your on-site location.

You Can Reveal More About Your Business on Social Media

These days, social media websites are where potential customers search when they want to learn more about a brand or a business. It is not surprising because these sites have a design that allows the business owners to share the most recent information about everything they offer from products and services to upcoming events.

Also, when someone is searching for something related tonight you offer, your business can come up as the answer to the search. It is made possible by the tools on social media that can index your activities and information by the search engines.

Social Media Is an Excellent Tool for Good Customer Service

Being able to provide good customer service is one of the strong points of any successful small business. While social media easily provides a two-way communication platform for you and your customers, it is also an excellent platform for you to improve the efficiency of your customer service and provide quick responses to your audience.

This way, it is more ensured that customer inquiries are not ignored, and your audience will be privier to the fact that you care about them and their experience with your brand.

When you establish social media for customer service and provide an instant response to their inquiries, you can meet business goals with ease. Current statistics have shown that businesses that handle their customer feedbacks well through social media earn more revenue by 20-40 percent more than others.

Social Media Improves the Efficiency of Your Email Marketing

Email marketing which is one of the ancient marketing techniques now has a new side to it because of the rise of social media. You can now cover more audience by sharing your email newsletter in all your social networks. This way, you are not limited to just your list of subscribers or followers. Your content can be seen now by a much larger and better-targeted audience, and you will get the kind of awareness that can drive sales.

You can also invite readers more readers and subscribers by adding a link on in your Facebook or other social pages for them.
Small businesses which have seized this opportunity and combined these groundbreaking tools have recorded a difference in marketing and have gotten a level playing ground to create more awareness for their business and improve their relationship with existing customers.

Everyone Uses Social Media

The larger population of Americans today uses smartphones. I'm in response to this development, a growing number of businesses are going the digital way and offering mobile-user experiences. The big social networks like Pinterest, Twitter, Instagram, and Facebook provide free to use mobile applications that enable business owners, and managers establish and maintain their online presence very easily. Small businesses indeed benefit a lot from the rising trend of mobile activity being a part of everyday life. Even better is the fact that mobile apps allow their users to connect to websites of their choice from anywhere.

User activities aren't limited to just sharing events from their personal lives. People also use their social networks to search for products, services, businesses and connect with brands.

Social media, especially when it is mobile friendly, is a great way to get awareness for your business or product because you can be found when someone is running a search on the go for something related.

Chapter 3:
Getting Started

In this chapter, we will be looking at the different strategies you can implement in growing your personal brand. These strategies are like those you incorporate in developing a business.

STRATEGIES FOR PERSONAL BRANDING

Find A Niche

A niche is a smaller part of a large industry which you choose to focus your personal brand. It is essential to select a niche to reach an audience that will have a genuine interest in what you have to offer. When selecting the right niche for your personal brand, there are a few questions you can answer:

- What do you love doing?

- Is there a group of people you enjoy working with?

- Do you prefer a specific industry?

- Can I make money in this niche?

- Is there a small part of that industry where the audience is not receiving enough attention?

- Do you think you can meet the needs of individuals within this small part?

If you can answer these questions, then you will find a good niche. I mean ALL the questions. You may be a professional lawyer, but you can't handle all types of cases. A criminal lawyer doesn't do the same job as a Personal Injury Lawyer.

During a niche selection, a lot of people make the mistake of choosing a category which will get them audiences from various areas. It voids the reason for a niche selection. The niche should be a small part of a much larger industry that will provide a targeted audience. You will not be able to appeal to anyone if you are trying to appeal to everyone. To further explain, consider an individual that performs game reviews.

The gaming industry covers sports, adventure, simulation, Massively Multiplayer Online (MMO), and many more categories. If you decide to build a brand within the gaming industry, you cannot appeal to everyone within the industry. The terms that apply to sports games differ from those that apply to MMOs.

Trying to review games from all categories implies that you will be unable to become an expert in a category. You won't be able to give an in-depth review of any category.

By focusing on a category, you can connect with the audience. Connecting with the audience will earn their trust. People will usually follow someone they trust. To be able to connect with the audience, you need to learn everything about them. You can start by answering the following questions:

- What daily struggles do they experience?

- What are the things they might think about?

- What are their beliefs?

- Is there anything that may prevent them from getting a good night's rest?

By getting to know your audience, you will be able to tailor your content to meet their needs.

Analyzing Your Competition

This analysis is in no way supposed to be a comparison. It is only a strategy which helps in identifying areas you can leverage for your success within a niche. Through this analysis, it is also possible to identify a niche that is oversaturated.

Having an excess competition and having no competition indicate that a niche is not the best option. When there is no competition, it implies that there is no target audience in need of content. Choose a niche with a few experts with a lot of room for you to grow. There should also be opportunities for your brand to stand out within the niche.

Understand Your Personal Brand

You can only know the expectations your target audience have if you have a clear understanding of the personal brand you are building. You will also can use these expectations to benefit your personal brand.

The first step is to learn what makes your brand indispensable. It can be a skill or multiple skills which your personal brand offers but no other brand does. As soon as you identify these skills, showcase them at every opportunity. Your personal brand is already being established on social media which makes it the best place to display your skills. It can be by posting helpful comments on different topics. You can also contribute to other pages in a niche that aligns with your other skills.

It is also vital you make everyone understand that you are available to help if the need arises. Always look to create opportunities for your personal brand. If you have unique skills which you are not showing to the world, you will become underrated and undervalued. It is not what you want for your personal brand. A personal brand that is underrated becomes the last option for the target audience. They do not expect much from you.

Creating A Brand Voice

The voice you choose for your personal brand determines how you interact with your audience. It also defines the response you get from the audience. There are different paths you can take when developing your brand voice. Your personal voice can be in any of the following formats:

- Authoritative

- Informative

- Friendly

- Conversational

- Technical

- Professional

As your personal brand develops, it becomes easier for the brand voice to evolve. Although this is an option, sticking to a unique brand voice is essential. The right brand voice will make it easy to form a connection with your audience.

Since your personal brand will include a lot of authentic posts, a consistent brand voice will make it easily recognizable. When your audience visits your profile on any platform, they will be expecting both a personality and a voice that is familiar.

Identify Your Target Audience

This is just a quick look since you will find a whole chapter on your target audience as you read on. The target audience is the foundation of your personal brand. It is essential you know the people you are trying to appeal to. As a personal brand, you will be able to identify your competitive advantage if you pick a target audience. It will help in improving the clarity of your brand message.

Understand the Importance of Making Connections

Your personal brand will feel the impact of the connections you make now and in the future. Creating a connection usually depends on the first impression you leave on a new member of your audience. The first thing you need to understand is that there is no do-over when it comes to first impressions.

Being intentional is an excellent way to steer an interaction to leave a good lasting impression. You can also use it to assess the image an individual has of your personal brand. Answering the following questions can help you get an idea of the impression your audience has about your brand:

- How many members of your target audience know about your personal brand?

- What do these members know about the personal brand?

- Is there anyone that doesn't know about your personal brand but can have a positive influence on the brand?

- Are you reaching individuals who can promote your brand in the future?

- Do you have a good relationship with top personal brands within your niche?

By considering the answers to these questions, it is possible to identify where you stand. Always keep this in mind when engaging with your audience. Each interaction should be able to promote your personal brand.

How Do You Establish Connections?

There are specific topics you can talk about within your niche which may give you the opportunity for a favorable interaction. Learning how to curate content to be beneficial to both your personal brand and the target audience is essential. Here is how you create great connections:

Your Profile Should Announce You

Building a personal brand will involve extensive use of various social media platforms. Each platform usually offers its users the opportunity to set up a profile. The profile contains some personal information which makes the user easy to find. When setting up your profile, it is crucial you highlight your unique skills and your niche. It makes it easy for other people within the niche to find you.

Be Informed

To make connections, having the latest information is necessary. The information you need includes any upcoming events, any online conversation within your niche, trending topics within your niche, as well as problems that need to be solved within your niche.

Learning about upcoming events and attending such events can provide the opportunity for one-on-one interactions with influencers within your niche. Posting your opinions on a trending topic will also give other online personal brands the opportunity to assess your expertise.

Make Your Own Opportunities

One of the simplest ways to create a connection is to make your own opportunities. Attending an industry event is an easy way to meet other people in the industry. Solving a common problem within your niche will also gain the attention of other personal brands and influencers within the niche. This will promote interaction with these influencers and brands.

Don't Write-Off the Competition

Your goal as a personal brand is to bring something different, a unique perspective, to the table. There is no better way to achieve this than to research the competition. The research will show you what they are doing, what they are not doing, areas of strengths as well as weakness. These are areas where you can identify pointers for improvements. You can also study the effectiveness of the processes which a competitor adopts.

Skills You Need to Develop When Building A Personal Brand

Writing Skills

Becoming an excellent writer is essential in creating a personal brand. As an excellent writer, you can curate content that will be pleasurable to your audience, offer clarity, and simplicity. You can follow any of these two paths to develop your writing skill:

- Working alongside an editor or writer with more experience: a lot of people have chosen to enlist the services of a ghostwriter when developing content. Although this method may prove to have its downsides later, it is an excellent place to start. You can opt for this method if you are having difficulties creating time to improve your personal writing skills.

- Train in writing content in English: Learning to write in plain English is the most effective way to develop your writing skills. English is a better language option since a broader audience understands it. It is also easier to find people who can translate your work to other languages if it is in English.

Become A Master at Public Speaking

To become successful in building a personal brand, you need to be confident when talking to other professionals within a niche as well as your audience. It is common for individuals to have a fear of public speaking. The most crucial step is trying to conquer this fear. Like how you perfect any other skill; you can master the art of public speaking by engaging in public speaking. By getting used to it, the fear will slowly fade away.

It is also important you don't mistake nervousness for fear. It is entirely reasonable for an individual to feel nervous before a speech. It affects even those you may consider masters in the art. To start, turn your focus to small groups. It can be in a peer support group, professional association, or a community gathering.

Effective Use Of SEO

An essential skill that a lot of people learn later is Search engine optimization. Regardless of its importance, it is relatively easy to understand. One or two days of study should be able to shape your writing.

There are still a few aspects which may be very difficult to learn, but the basics are quite easy to grasp. One of the most challenging parts of the SEO process is finding the right keywords. It must be a keyword that is relevant, has a large search volume, an easily rank at the top of google search results. There are a lot of online resources available to learn more about SEO optimization.

Email Marketing

Sending a personal email is not the same as Email marketing. A subscription to an email service provider is necessary to make use of email marketing. These providers include Constant Contact and Mail-Chimp. To get the most out of this service, you should avoid using desktop email clients such as Outlook.

Developing your email marketing skill involves learning the basics of sending an email broadcast. You will also need a clear understanding of the analytics, segmentation, automated drip campaigns, and personalization.

Chapter 4:
Understanding Your Target Audience

What Is A Target Audience?

A target audience is a unique group of individuals who have similar characteristics. Individuals who make up this group are those who are likely going to show interest in the services or products you offer. There are different ways to narrow down your target audience. It includes any of the following:

- Income

- Gender

- Profession

- Age

- Marital status

- Location

- Level of education

Why Is It So Important?

The importance of having a target audience is quite simple. Being effective in creating your content is necessary. It is more useful to appeal to a specific group of individuals with similar interests. Importance of connecting with your audience

Loyalty

Forming an understanding with your target audience is one of the best ways to gain their loyalty. Through this understanding, it is possible to learn about their needs and offer services that will cater to these needs.

Since there will be consistency in the high-quality services, your target audience keeps patronizing your brand. As your reputation grows, there will also be confidence and trust. It is how you can establish loyalty.

Reduced Marketing Effort

An understanding between you and your audience will solidify the connection between both parties. As you foster this connection, it will lead to a client base consisting of your regular audience members. Having a client base minimizes the additional costs you will need to spend when marketing new services and products. Your client base will also be willing to assist in referring your brand to attract new customers.

Brand Advocates

Through an understanding of the basic requirements of your audience, it is easier to satisfy them. Continuous satisfaction can turn your audience into your brand advocates. As brand advocates, your audience will recommend and promote your brand to others. It means you get free marketing that increases your brand awareness and reputation.

Effective Targeting

Connecting with your audience makes it possible to advertise to them effectively. It will be easy to learn about the social media platforms they use, the kind of entertainment that interests them, and what moves them to take actions.

Through the results of your findings, it is possible to tailor your content to your audience to produce the impact you desire. Your audience will only listen if they find meaning within your message. A good connection with your audience also makes it possible to pitch new ideas to them.

How to Improve Exposure and Conversions

Contacting Niche Bloggers and Vloggers

There are lots of other social media pages that have a large following that you can connect. It can also be a vlog or a blog. If you have a product you sell, you can reach out to such individuals to make a sponsored post.

The sponsored post is another easy way to connect with other users who have an interest in your products. Although this is like what you do when building your personal brand, you are sharing your products with a fan base different from yours.

Popular sponsored posts which are available on YouTube are "unboxing" videos. Such videos show a YouTuber unbox a product, tell users about the product, and try out the product for users to see. It is a cheaper means of getting more viewers to look at your product. This method is quite affordable when considering the kind of exposure, it offers.

Using Targeted Advertisements

Social media makes it very easy to post ads online. As a result, a lot of users have become blind to most of the ads that appear. It is why you need to implement targeted advertisements. Through the interests or demographic information of users, it is possible to post an ad which will be relevant to the user. By incorporating targeted ads in your brand building strategy, you can expand your reach to a broader audience.

Using A Referral System

Networking is a crucial part of your personal brand. By growing your network, you can reach more individuals. A referral system is one of the few methods available to expand this network. In this system, users have a unique referral code that they can give out to other individuals. By giving out this referral code, they can attract new prospects which you otherwise would not be able to reach.

There should be an incentive that will make users more likely to give out this code. It can be in the form of a discount on their next purchase or a commission. Regardless of what form the offer takes, it should be valuable enough to prompt users to share the code. A low offer will not provide the motivation that users need. As a result, you may have a low yield.

Partnering with Other Brands

Your personal brand can gain a lot from a partnership with a larger company in the market. The company doesn't have to compete with your brand. The good idea is to pick a company that complements the services you offer your viewers.

In a way, the partnership must be mutually beneficial to both parties. An easy way to explain this partnership is to consider a YouTuber who performs video game reviews on YouTube. This individual may have the opportunity to partner with a larger gaming studio that provides certain resources. It can be in the form of free versions of a new game while the YouTuber offers a gameplay review to subscribers. There are other forms of partnership which are a lot easier to understand.

Attend Events

Most of the work you will be doing when building your personal brand will be online. Nonetheless, you should also remember to take advantage of traditional methods. In this case, look out for events around you that you can attend. The event may be a festival, convention, seminar, or conference where you can display your products and services. Directly engaging with other participants during such events can be very beneficial.

Guest Blogging

Establishing yourself as an expert creates a lot of openings for you to grow your audience. One of such openings is the opportunity to become a guest blogger. Guest blogging is a method through which you increase traffic to your site by writing a content which you post on another blog. The blog you write for will usually be one which is within your niche.

The main benefit of guest blogging is that you gain access to the viewers on the blog where you post the content. You also can post links that redirect back to your site. If you decide to participate in guest blogging, quality is paramount. The quality of the content you are posting on the blog should be of high standards to attract new viewers to your blog. It is also vital you guest blog on blogs that have targeted following.

Creating written content is more common, but there are a few companies that may want videos. You should jump at these opportunities.

The exposure you get from videos is usually a lot more than written content offers.

How to Identify Opportunities to Grow Your Audience

When you need to identify opportunities for audience growth, it can be through quantitative or qualitative research.

Quantitative Research

It is a form of research which depends on numerical data. The research offers an opportunity for you to learn about the strengths of competitors as well as the weaknesses you can use to your advantage.

Quantitative research provides opportunities to find areas where you can grow your audience from better understanding of customer demographics. Although it usually contains a lot of statistical information, it is crucial you don't rely solely on the data. You need to combine the other forms of information available to make more beneficial changes. Quantitative research includes the following:

- Product sales number

- Financial trends

- Questionnaires

Qualitative Research

Qualitative research is an easy way to learn about customer interests, trends in the industry which have been poorly implemented, as well as attitudes and views of customers. You can perform qualitative research through any of the following methods:

- A review of your competitors to learn about their customer services as well as products

- Creating focus groups that consist of both potential customers as well as you true customers

- Conversations, both formal and informal, with your customers

Qualitative research data is not as easy to interpret as quantitative research data. By identifying the trends, you can implement, it is possible to attract more clients to your personal brand. To further understand how to gain information from quantitative and qualitative research, you should assess different areas of your personal brand.

Assessing Your Audience

To understand the behavior of your prospects, it is crucial you assess your audience. Some of the information you will gain from this assessment include how your brand influences the audience, how the audience evaluates your brand, and how they get information regarding the brand. To assess your audience, you need to combine various research methods such as:

- Surveys and interviews of customers

- Analytics

- Keyword research

- Analysis of user-generated content

- Brand immersion

With these methods, it is possible to create a profile for an individual within the audience. It also allows you to adjust your strategy to suit the profile.

Assessing the Trends

When developing your content strategy, the "what" aspect is important. Evaluating the trends can help in the definition of this aspect.

During this assessment, you will need to gather contents with the most engagement within your niche and analyze this content. You will also need to analyze patterns in this content. Once your analysis is complete, it is possible to identify areas where you can improve your content strategy to attract more of your target audience. Here are some methods which are beneficial when assessing trends:

- Analysis of resources cited

- Identifying subtopics

- Sentiment analysis

- Analysis of quoted experts

- Determining the angle

- Analysis of compelling questions

Through these research methods, it becomes possible to understand what makes why your target audience interacts with content, questions they are likely to answer, as well as content they share and cite.

Assessing the Media

By evaluating the media, you can discover other personal brands within your niche that attract the most of your target audience. Combining the results of your media assessment to the results of your trends assessment, you have a better understanding of how to develop content that will gain the attention of the audience.

- Assessing the media should include the following methods:

- Analysis of social engagement

- Analysis of industry experts

- Analysis of paid media

- Analysis of social influencers in your industry

- Analysis of industry publications

All these are content sources in an industry. By analyzing these sources, you can promote your content more effectively.

Assessing the Competition

Both in business and a personal brand, there is always a competitor. Your competition is the main reason why you are making your brand unique.

By assessing the competition, you can spot new opportunities for growth that is not being leveraged by your competitors. Assessing the competition includes the following:

- Evaluating SEO optimization

- Analyzing the navigation and architecture of social media pages

- Content inventory

- Analysis of keyword gap

Through the competition assessment, you can better understand the reason for specific actions.

How to Assess the Competition

To successfully evaluate your competition, you need to identify the competition. You need to have a list of these competitors. Creating this list is quite easy – look for personal brands within the niche you have chosen. The next step is to identify the strengths and weaknesses of each competitor. It involves taking note of what makes each competitor unique, the services or experience they offer their audience and areas where they are lacking.

Taking note of the keywords each competitor is using and those they avoid can also be very helpful. Also, identify the platforms where their audience can find them and those where they have no presence. Now that you have done your research on the competition, it is time to look at your brand. What are the things that you can do differently? What strengths do you have that separate you from your competition?

You should have a separate slide for each competitor, so your work is easy. List all the findings under each competitor and state your recommendations on how to make your brand better. The date of the research is crucial. So much can change in a short time.

A Quick Summary

Growth opportunities for your audience become easy to identify when you spot the needs of your target audience which are not currently being satisfied by your personal brand or other brands within your niche.

Your ability to notice growing trends in the form of weak signals will also be useful in leveraging an opportunity before it blooms into a more significant trend on which your competition can jump on. Niche communities, social listening, and industry buzz can help in noticing these weak signals.

Chapter 5:
How to Make Your Brand Unique

For you to stand out from the crowd, the first step is to accept the things that make you unique. It is common to find a lot of people with unique traits that blend with the crowd. Others create an image for themselves and stand out.

It is essential you avoid shaping your persona to fit societal labels. Accepting the things that make you different will make it possible to control how your life. There are different areas where individuals are unique. These aspects can also help in shaping the brand they develop. Some of the important aspects include the following:

Experiences
The experiences an individual will have throughout their lifetime will differ from those any other individual will have. It doesn't matter if you grow up in the same home or spend a lot of time together with a person.

Your experiences in life also serve as huge turning points as you grow. It can be your biggest failure, your most embarrassing moment, a choice you make, or a moment when you had your most significant success. These experiences shape the person you have become and are some of the things that make you unique.

Creativity

It is another important aspect which makes each person unique. The creative ability of an individual is entirely different from the other. In some individuals, it is the ability to invent a new product while in others, it is the ability to develop a way to carry out a task.

Creativity can be further subdivided into talents that include the visionary, inventor, adventurer, pilot, explorer, navigator, poet, and diplomat. This is according to Lynne Levesque, Ed. D.

Perception

Everyone has a unique perception of life. It is a unique way you view different happenings around you. It also affects the experiences you will have.

Creating A Brand That Is Unique

Make a list of the exclusive offers your brand has for its clients. Let your offer to the market distinguish you from other brands including those with higher capitals. For your brand to stand out in the very competitive market of today, you need to carry out a careful study of what society requires that no one is offering. Pay rapt attention to the quality of the product and services your brand has to offer.

The first step to take is to carefully select your target audience and give them something different from what other similar brands as yours are offering. Even better, let your services and product be in line with improving the lives of your customers in ways such as;

- Providing better options at an affordable rate

- Improved customer service

- Improving productivity

- Stress relieves on daily activity

- Time management

Let there be a balance among knowledge, passion, and profitability. You hear people talk about choosing a niche to focus like it is something straightforward to do. There is a wide range of niches one can decide to focus on, but it could be a little bit of a challenge to find one that catches your interest, you're knowledgeable in, and you can monetize. Therefore, before choosing a niche to focus on ensure those critical factors are not missing.

Be Different but Real

Let your brand show people the real you; this is because no matter how hard you try people can always identify fake. Other than doing what every other person is doing, think of new outstanding ideas and offer it to the society.

Ask yourself a question, if you quit today what would be the reaction of your customers. What is that unique offer of yours your customer would miss the most when you decide to quit today? Your answer to this question is the most valuable selling point of your brand.

Be Human

There is more to it than just standing out, be human as well. It is essential to see your client and competitor as the humans they are, therefore strive to build a good customer relationship with the clients.

Do Not Be Overly Money Conscious

Instead of choosing your area of focus based on money, do something you love. It might take a long while to monetize your passion, but it's sure better than forcing yourself to belong to a niche you know nothing about and have zero passion for. It will save you from wasting time and effort and probably ending up depressed and worn out.

Do Not Force It

It could be tempting to follow a trend and what others are doing but that might not play out well for you. It is best to focus on something you are well grounded in and passionate about; this will give you a better chance at achieving success.

Stay True to Yourself

Reach out to people already in the same niche you wish to go into, learn from them and share the knowledge you have with them as well.

Show the world the real you and what you have to offer. Do not imitate or try to be like someone else; originality is key to success. If you feel you can't survive in a niche choose another.

Create Your Buyer Persona

Do not be a "jack of all trade, master of none" kind of brand. It is better to have one job correctly done than have several poor ones. Maintaining focus on one thing gives trust in your brand. To do this, you can get free templates online that would help you create a good buyer persona for your clients.

Decide on what your Value-Add would be. Identify that unique skill or quality you possess that will make your brand stand out and capitalize on it. Every individual has something unique about them, figure yours out and offer it to the society.

Talk to Those Close to You

It is easier to know more about yourself, your strength and weakness from those closest to you. Talk to your colleagues, friends, and family and find out what they think about you. Request that they be plain with you and hold nothing back. By so doing you would come to discover things you probably didn't know about yourself.

Know and Trust in Yourself

We sometimes pass through the trial and error process to decide which niche to focus on. Base your decision on passion, skill, and knowledge. The moment this is determined, work with it and create a unique brand that truly defines you.

Personalize It

A unique brand is most often than not personal. It defines the face behind the brand, the individual's communication skills, interest, values and lots more. Your brand must have something captivating to offer to the public, or you leave them indifferent towards you. Always apply this rule to your business, "stand apart by standing out."

Analyze Your Competitors

Study your competitors, find out what they are currently talking about, what is trending online and what the market expects from your sector. Go deeper into topics other brands are ignoring and create something unique out of it for your brand.

Who Are You?

Do not alter your identity to fit in; no one can be more you than you. If you wish to retain your customers or client, it is essential that you stay genuine to yourself as people can easily see through fakeness. Do not lose yourself in a bid to do what others are doing.

Create A Unique Blueprint for Your Brand

Creating the perfect blueprint for your brand that will speak to your audience and tell them who you are, there are three important exercises you must carry out. First, make a list of what the market needs the most, then make a list of your best skills, and finally make a list of your greatest passion. Create your brand blueprint around the top choices from each list. Below is a list of areas every business should focus on for growth.

Channel Strengths

Create a platform whereby people can easily access your brand; your availability should play out in your favor. Seeks out other options that would help widen your reach online, you can try promoting your brand on various social media channel. A change in environment or platform could be the change your platform needs to move forward. However, because change brings about different reactions to ensure that your content is of high value or you risk losing your customers.

Product Strength

Rather than focusing majorly on technical supremacy, pay more attention to the quality of your product. The quality of your product will speak better for your brand and keep you ahead of others in your industry. When people build trust in your brand as a result of the quality services you offer, you become a force to be reckoned with.

People Strengths

Think of those qualities that made you choose your employees and use it to your advantage. Encourage them to put in more effort and do better than they have in the past. Figure out ways by which you can bring out the best in them to achieve the desired result. You can accomplish this by giving them a more complex task than they have previously handled. Study your team, find out their strength and max-imize it to the advantage of your brand. Hire an HR team with the capacity to choose very efficient employees.

Competitive Strengths

Raise the bar so high that your competitors will struggle to measure up with. However, you need a team of highly efficient people to pull this through. Give your team the task to achieve an outrageous vision within a limited period. Let this task be an upgrade to the brand vision that you need to implement rather than as a new goal. It will cause your team to figure out better strategies to achieve this and in turn help build individual strength. Provide useful resources and opportu-nities for your team and train them on how to handle the task ahead. It gives your team the impression that what you require of them is achievable. Build the strength of your brand from the inside to achieve the desired result.

Awareness Strengths

Give the market something specific to make them remember you. With the high rate of competition in the world today, it requires significant effort to stand. Study your target market and your competitors and find out what you can do to make your brand preferable to others. Do something that will increase your visibility on social media platforms. Stay active on the channels where you experience better visibility and let your presence be felt. Find out the areas of your business that requires improvement to boost your visibility. Focus on inclination more than demographics.

Adaptive Strengths

Do you find it easy to adapt to changes? If yes, in what ways can you best utilize this attribute to the betterment of your business? Identifying and accepting changes rapidly can be an added advantage to your business especially if you specialize in a highly competitive niche. It will make your brand stand out as that brand that brings about the change the market desires. Your brand is appreciated for daring to move along with the trend, and your customers are usually the first to benefit from this change. Therefore, because you were bold enough to bring about change you become a leading brand in your industry and command the respect of others. It is vital to ensure you do not move faster than appropriate all in the bid to over-impress people; this could hurt your brand. Moving along with trend gives you the edge to get investors who are looking to invest in something new. Your pace to adapting to changes must be beneficial to your cause, or you stand the risk of falling out.

Chapter 6:
Creating A Personal Brand on YouTube

What Is YouTube?

On the internet today, YouTube remains the most popular video sharing platform available. As a registered user on the platform, you will have the opportunity to share video content. Anyone who visits the site will be able to access and watch the videos. Some of the key functions of YouTube include the following:

- Uploading videos to a channel

- Using keywords to search for videos

- Watching videos

- Posting comments, liking, and sharing videos from other users

- Creating playlists of similar videos

- Subscribing to YouTube Channels

- Gaining subscribers on your channel

What Makes YouTube Useful?

As a video sharing platform which is free to use, YouTube offers a lot of educational videos. It is a platform where users can discover new ideas. Helpful, instructional videos are also available for users. Some of the video contents available on the site include how-to guides, hacks, music videos, recipes, comedy shows, game reviews, and more. It is also a great platform for vloggers to showcase their creativity.

THE VALUE OF YOUTUBE

It Offers A Large Traffic

YouTube remains one of the most important online video sharing platforms available. Daily, people view over 3 billion videos on the platform. It is a clear indication of the traffic on the platform.

Using YouTube to build your personal brand also implies that you will have access to this high traffic. It also becomes effortless to reach your target audience. There are other significant advantages which you can enjoy from the traffic on YouTube. These include the following:

- The ease with which you can locate your target audience and individuals who are likely going to become your fans

- There are over 1 billion users who pay to enjoy YouTube videos every month

- It becomes easier for people to locate your personal brand as it is the 2nd largest search engine in the world

- Maintaining consistency and offering high-quality content which solves a significant issue of a viewer will earn their loyalty

It Improves Your Visibility on Google

If you type in a keyword into a Google search panel, you will notice that videos also come up. The Google search results are usually a combination of these videos along with images, books, news, and more. It is a good way to ensure that you find the most relevant information available on the internet.

The number of videos that show up alongside text-only pages goes to show how important videos are becoming. In building your personal brand, YouTube can help you take advantage of this growing trend.

The best way to leverage this opportunity is to create high-quality written content which you can then complement with a high-quality video on YouTube. The written content may be on your blog or social media platform with a direct link to your YouTube page. It will increase your personal brand appearance on Google search results. Incorporating YouTube into your personal brand building strategy will also establish your brand authority within your niche. Setting yourself as an expert will even get you noticed by Google. It then makes it possible for your page ranking on search results to rise.

Re-purposing Your Content

Re-purposing content is very beneficial since it helps in saving both time and money. It is also very efficient when you are trying to market your content. It is a lot easier to reach your target audience since it is the type of content that meets their specifications. If you run a blog, some of the formats that are available for re-purposing content include:

- Video Series

- Podcasts

- Presentations

Through re-purposing of content, you can develop a single idea into about four content formats. It makes it possible to reach a wider audience with improvements in engagement.

YouTube Helps You Create an Email List

Providing content which is valuable and engaging offers an opportunity to increase your email list. You can find a software that allows users sign-up to the email list from the video. This software will stop the video for a short time so that the user can add an email address to subscribe to the list.

It is an easy and stress-free method of growing your email list. Remember, it will only be useful if you offer high-quality and engaging content. Your Viewers Will Help in Promoting You and Purchase from You. Conversions are possible through videos on YouTube. If there is a personal touch that connects with the viewer, they are more likely going to make a purchase. Connecting with them on an emotional scale will build trust between both parties.

It Offers the Option to Monetize Your Channel

Using Google AdSense video program is an easy way to earn money you're your YouTube videos. It is usually available if you can consistently upload high-quality videos. The earnings on your channel can enter six-figures annually if you use it correctly. It is a combination of your earnings from the Google AdSense as well as what you aid from paid adverts. Don't think you are the first to learn about AdSense – there are over 20 million YouTube channels already benefitting from the program.

Become A Global Sensation

The reach you get from YouTube is quite phenomenal. Since it is a video sharing platform, people from various parts of the world find it easy to identify your brand. Authorizing support for subtitles on YouTube will also allow you to share content with viewers regardless of the language barrier. Consistently uploading videos will open doors for new viewers from these locations. The option of including a closed caption will also enable you to connect with viewers with unique requirements.

Closed captions have become an essential part of YouTube videos. According to research, videos with closed caption have a 4% increase in the number of views and subscribers. Including a Call-to-Action is a great way to promote your personal brand through YouTube. Adding links to other videos, services, and other social pages also help.

You Will Have More Visibility on Search Engines

Since Google includes videos and images to its search results, YouTube can help improve the visibility of your personal brand. Uploading videos regularly with new content in each video will improve your chances of appearing in a search result.

Proper use of metadata is one factor that affects the outcome in this case. Google and other search engines pick up metadata when selecting results which will be relevant to the search entry. Creating a blog post on a topic and then providing a link to the video is also very helpful. The link should direct the viewers to your YouTube channel.

CREATING A STRONG YOUTUBE PRESENCE

Promote

Another way to drive traffic to your YouTube channel is by promoting the channel on other social media platforms. The first step is to post short clips on different social media profiles. If the video offers high-quality content, viewers will be looking to watch it till the end.

Adding a link is also important. It is the only way you can redirect the traffic to your channel. It also prevents the competition from getting the attention of your viewers while they try to locate your channel.

You should also get your viewers to subscribe to your channel. It improves the chances of your videos appearing on the YouTube homepage. Including metadata will also promote video optimization. Add keywords to these descriptions to enhance effectiveness. Video optimization also promotes your channel on Google as they become more noticeable in search results.

Selecting A Featured Video

Your featured video is the first video that appears to any user that opens your channel homepage. Why not make it your best? It is important you choose a video which has a high-quality recording, is relevant, entertaining, and short. These features are self-explanatory. To appeal to users, you should try to change this video often. A title that attracts viewers is also crucial for your featured video. A thumbnail which best depicts the video is also essential.

Customize Your Channel

The appearance of your channel can also make it unique. The aesthetic you choose when customizing the channel should reflect the brand. Colors and logos that your audience can associate with your brand should be used in the videos.

Create A Schedule

While building your personal brand, you may not have enough resources to hire people to manage your social media accounts. So, you must make the most of your time.

Creating a schedule and following it will help in creating content which is fresh and of high-quality. It, in turn, attracts the target audience you have in mind. Starting a series of how-to videos makes it easy to come up with a new idea for the next video. It also attracts the target audience in anticipation for the next video in the series.

Reply Comments

On YouTube, users can comment after a video or also drop a comment on the homepage of your channel. Administrators on YouTube have the power to disable comments, moderate them, or allow the comments. It applies to both a video and the channel.

To moderate a comment after it has been posted, you can remove it from the comments section or report as spam. Keep an eye on the comments below your videos or the channel homepage. It makes it possible to identify conversations that deserve a response. There should be a standard for deleting comments. Just because a comment is negative doesn't mean it shouldn't be on the post. Removing comments with foul language or words that are offensive is allowed.

Put Related Content in A Playlist

When a user is searching for any content that is relevant to the video they just finished watching, a playlist can assist. The playlist allows users to access another video content on the channel page easily. Through the playlist, it is possible for a viewer to keep watching videos without having to select the play button on the page. Creating labels that accurately describe the content of the videos within a playlist is very important.

Use the Analytics

On your YouTube channel, there is analytics. It includes engagement data such as the number of shares, comments, likes, and so on. Performance data and demographic data are also available on a per-video basis. Taking time to assess the information can help you decide on the usefulness of the content on your channel. It also helps to determine areas where you can make improvements to attract more subscribers and viewers.

Niche Selection Strategies

Selecting a niche for your YouTube channel is another aspect you need to cover. Having a good niche strategy is also essential if you want to avoid making any decision you may regret later. In this section, you will find some useful tips which you can use in shaping your niche selection strategy.

What Do You Have A Passion For? What Are You Great At?

Your passion is always an excellent focus on your channel. It is an area where you are likely going to have the most experience as well as confidence.

You can start by listing out all the things you do well. Areas where you show exceptional talent should be at the top of this list. It is an excellent time to be proud of some all these talents. Being an expert in a field may not be the focus when selecting a niche. It should be a subtle blend of your talents and your passion that will decide a niche where you will stand out. As you begin to build yourself within a niche, you will slowly grow to become an expert.

When you sit down and think about a video, how many topics come to mind? Any number less than ten shows that this is not the best niche for you. It only shows that getting inspiration to run the channel within that niche will be very difficult. Are there changes that will affect your passion for this niche? Is it a passion that will change in a few years? Assessing your answers to this question can help you better understand your passion.

A video that is useful to a subscriber will make them visit more often. You may consider building a channel within the entertainment niche. Although viewers may enjoy getting a good laugh, they will still opt for a channel that can provide useful information they can apply to their daily activities. Channels that make the most money are usually those that provide information which both investors and viewers consider being helpful.

Does Your Potential Niche Have an Audience?

If you can pick out a niche that you are moving towards, you must ensure that there are people who will watch your videos. It means that there should be a target audience for the niche. There will be certain subjects you will need to cover within a niche. Is there an audience searching for these topics? If there is, then you are going to get people to view your videos. You should perform quick research to see how much people search for the niche you have chosen. An excellent place to start is the Google AdWords Keyword Planner. It shows the monthly searches which a keyword gets on the average.

Google Trends is another vital tool. It shows the popularity of a topic over a period. With this tool, you can know if a niche is only popular at a specific time during the year as well as changes in demand with time.

What Is the Competition Like Within the Niche and What Do They Offer?

The competition in a niche will determine the difficulty when building your brand within the niche. A simple look at the number of active YouTubers within the niche will give you a clear idea. A niche that is full of YouTubers will be challenging when starting. Being flexible with your niche choices will make it easy to find one with less competition. It is crucial that the niche is in high demand. So, you are searching for a low competition with high demand niche in this case.

If you are already building a personal brand on other social media platforms, this is not an option. Using targeting keywords will help in a competitive niche. Although things will be a lot more difficult, you can still reach your goals. You also need to analyze what the other YouTubers in the niche are doing. Learn about the content they offer. Also, learn how they promote engagement on their channel. Reading through comments from their audience can show you some of the flaws in their content and where you can make improvements. You must remain authentic and unique in your approach.

How Will You Stand Out Within the Niche?

High-quality content is not enough to keep your viewers interested. You must be skillful in how you make the presentation. Making the content fun for your viewers is also vital.

Your viewers will drop you for someone who offers the same high-quality content but with more entertainment. Adding some personality to your videos will make it unique and more entertaining. Some easy steps to take to add entertainment to a video include:

- Working on your introduction

- Improving the way, you speak

- Your appearance

- The concept of the video

- Visual effects

Making a few changes to these areas can bring a new theme and style to your videos. You need to be very creative in making changes if you want to stand out from your competition.

How Profitable Is the Niche?

Although your initial goal is to create your brand, making money from this brand is the long-term goal. It is why you need to consider the profitability of a niche before selecting one.

- Is there any side hustle available within the niche?

- Are there companies willing to sponsor the use and review of their products?

These are questions that can help you determine a niche that will be profitable. Receiving a sponsorship is not as easy as it sounds. Nonetheless, it is precious if you can land one. You can choose to become an affiliate as a side hustle which will earn you passive income.

Using the Trends

The visibility of your videos as well as the number of views can increase significantly if the content relates to a trending topic. Since a lot of viewers will be searching for trending topics daily, you are sure to get noticed by a lot of users. With trending topics, the earlier you use it to your advantage, the better. Since users may learn a lot about the subject within a day or two, the trend may die out before you can attract viewers. Below are some of the steps you can follow to get the most out of a trend:

Use Metadata

Adding metadata to a video is possible when you are about to upload the video on YouTube. The metadata is information relating to the video such as the title, tags, and description. Including the trending keyword in each metadata will promote the visibility of the video.

Find A Way to Increase Engagement

One of the main benefits of a trending topic is that it offers the opportunity to improve engagement with your viewers. Engagement is also an easy way to increase viewership and subscriptions. Simply asking a question or making a request during the video can get you the engagement you desire. Simple statements such as:

- How do you feel about this development? Leave a comment for us to know your thoughts

- If you love this video, remember to subscribe so you can be the first to learn about new posts!

Improving the Ranking of Your Videos

As the largest video sharing platform, there are various stats which make YouTube seem difficult for new channels. The platform has many videos and channels. To create equilibrium, it also has many users and visitors. So how do you make sure you reach your audience during a search? Your video needs to have a lot of likes, views, and shares for it to appear at the top of the results during a search. It is how the YouTube algorithm identifies trending content.

Steps to Take to Improve Your Video Ranks

There are some steps you can take to push your videos up the rankings. These steps will increase the views, likes, and shares which your video will get. As soon as there is a growth in these numbers, it becomes easy to notice an increase in the video rankings.

Offer High-Quality Content

Content is the most critical factor when developing a personal brand. It remains a crucial factor across all social media platforms. You can quickly identify the importance of great content by watching some of the top videos on YouTube. After watching these videos, you will notice that they have high-quality content which attracts the audience, improves engagement through comments and likes, while also promoting shares and subscription.

The only way you will be motivated to make more high-quality videos is when you can get more views on a previous post. By offering great content, you are going to solidify your relationship with your audience over a long period. In a case where there is significant competition in your niche, you can only stand out and survive by offering high-quality content in your videos. In simpler terms, the information you provide, scripts, flow, facts, and video quality need to be the best. It doesn't matter if your videos focus on humor, games, reviews, or makeup. By providing excellent video content, you can connect easily with your target audience.

Short Videos Are Better

Do you create videos that last an hour? Who will be willing to watch a video for that long? Unless it's a movie, you won't be able to grab the attention of your target audience. It is common knowledge that the attention span of individuals nowadays is quite short so why not use it to your advantage? Developing the first minute of your video to contain a lot of high-quality information is also essential. If you are unable to make an impression in the first minute, your viewer will move on to the next before you have that opportunity again. When building a personal brand on YouTube, you need to start with short videos. As the number of subscribers begins to increase, you can that gradually increase the duration of your videos. At this time, you have already gained the trust of your viewers.

Incorporate SEO

Through SEO optimization, it becomes easier for people to find your channel in the search results. Although the way you implement SEO optimization may differ in the content format, it still has the same effect. When uploading videos to your YouTube channel, you need to create your title according to SEO standards. It is also essential you add a description, URL, and tags to the video. It is the easiest way to enhance the ranking of your video.

Come Up with A Unique Concept

Delivering fresh content is the only way you are going to retain the loyalty of your audience. No one will be able to remain loyal to a page that keeps posting a video that they have seen so many times. Regardless of the humor, entertainment, or emotions, a video can produce at first; its effects will dwindle when you view it a second or third time.

It is common to find a lot of YouTubers who stepped into the limelight due to a unique concept which they incorporated. It is also very common to see a lot of other people trying to replicate these concepts to get them into the spotlight. It is a severe error which a lot of people make. Just because it produced the right results with a person doesn't imply that it will work for you. A significant downside to taking this line of action is the loss of authenticity when developing your content.

Another significant downside to copying others is the loss of members of your audience. The members you lose in this case may never return to your channel again. A lot of people may feel that this limits their ability to grow. It is a common misconception that arises when the competition is high within a niche. All you need is to ensure you have the proper experience, create your concept and style which separates you from the competition.

Look for Ways to Increase Your Subscribers

Your subscribers also play a crucial role in your video rankings. Having many subscribers will increase the number of shares, views, and likes on your videos. It will, in turn, improve the ranking of your video. It is essential you put in more effort to get people to subscribe to your channel. Reminding viewers subscribe to your channel and like your videos is important.

Chapter 7:
Creating A Personal Brand on Facebook

Getting Started

Should you build your personal brand with a Facebook Profile or Facebook Page? The answer to this question will depend on your preferences. There are certain areas where a Facebook Page offers advantages over a Facebook profile. It is also true when the roles are reversed.

When comparing organic reach and paid reach, using a Facebook profile offers a higher organic reach. A Facebook page is a better option when it comes to paid reach. You should also note that access to paid reach and advertising is no longer available on Facebook profiles. Facebook Pages also provide the analytics option to users. Analytics on Facebook is available in the form of Facebook Insights. The Insights tab is only available on the Pages.

Attracting your target audience also varies for both. Interaction with your target audience is much more comfortable with a Facebook profile. It gives you the option of interacting with friends and even converse with people who are in a group. Having many fans is vital for a

Facebook Page. It is only through engagement and a large fan base that a Facebook page can impress your target audience. A Facebook profile also provides interaction with the target audience.

If you need access to the various parts of Facebook, a profile is your best option. You can interact with other users on Facebook pages, groups, or profiles. With a Facebook page, you can post a comment in a group or on different profiles.

Setting Up Your Account

Optimize What Everyone Can See

Four parts of your Facebook account are visible to all other Facebook users. By making information from these parts' public, Facebook makes it very easy for other users to find your account. These parts are the:

- Profile picture

- Timeline cover photo

- Name of your Facebook profile that appears at the top

- Account URL or Facebook custom username

By taking the time to customize these areas, you can get more users to view your account. Here are steps to take to optimize your account: a name that is easy to remember.

When setting up your profile, Facebook requires users to do so using their real name. Nonetheless, users get to decide the name that appears at the top part of the profile. A nickname that is easy to remember and defines your brand is an excellent option in this case.

Profile Photo

Since there is no privacy protection setting for this profile photo, it is visible to all Facebook users. It is important that the picture you choose is professional and friendly. You can use a picture of yourself at an event that relates to your brand.

A Distinct Username

The number of Facebook users worldwide makes it challenging to choose a username. It is why you need to get creative. Come up with unique a name which is meaningful to your personal brand. You also need a username which you can incorporate into your business card, email signature, and URL.

Timeline Cover Photo

As soon as a user opens your page, the cover photo is the first image they see. It covers a large part of the screen. There are lots of benefits you can gain if you use the right cover photo. To set up a great cover photo, you should use a banner size of 851 x 315 pixels. The image should also reflect your brand.

STEPS TO TAKE WHEN BUILDING YOUR PERSONAL BRAND ON FACEBOOK

Adjust Your Privacy Settings.

There is a limit to the type of contents you can allow on your page. Since you are building a personal brand, you first must decide if a piece of information should be on your Facebook page. The privacy settings on Facebook allow you to set up restrictions on your page. These restrictions include limiting access to parts of your accounts to only Facebook friends. There are other parts which need to be accessible by all Facebook users. Building a personal brand means you need to make new connections. Information about your education, work, and success should be open to the public. It makes it possible to attract people who share your interests and those who work in a similar field.

The privacy settings also help you control what posts users can tag back to your page. Tagging on Facebook allows users to link a post directly to another account. Blocking the tagging feature doesn't prevent a post from appearing on the platform. Nonetheless, it becomes complicated for your followers to relate it to your page. It is also vital you avoid leaking too much personal information.

What Is Your Story?

The main reason why you are starting a personal brand is to influence other users. There should be a story behind it. It is a story you must be willing to tell. Anyone who decides to follow your personal brand will want to be a part of the brand. One way to make them feel like a part is to let them know the story behind the brand.

A story that offers both encouragement and motivation have the most impact. These are two things your followers need you to provide. Why you are taking this path and your experiences along the line help in shaping your story, and allows your followers to get familiar with you, while also making it easier for them to follow your brand all the way.

Avoid Spamming

Spamming is very common on Facebook, and most Facebook users hate it. I said most since I can't speak for people who spam. To prevent spamming, Facebook also tries its best to improve some of the security features available on the platform. Nonetheless, you should avoid making your contents look like spam when building a personal brand on Facebook. According to the terms of service on Facebook, you need permission for third-party advertisements on pages. It is why you need to take care when posting links on your page.

Another way you may be appearing as a spammer is by being inauthentic. It may be a simple error of sharing too many links or articles without verifying the authenticity of the source. It may also be as a result of articles which you post which may be an edit of a previous article you have written. Posting different URLs to the same article is also a form of spamming. You need to make sure you don't make such mistakes.

Expand Your Network

Expanding your network is always a vital part of building your personal brand on a social media platform. On Facebook, it is possible to import new contacts from your phonebook. Other channels like instant messenger and email accounts also offer this feature. Repeating this process every month is an easy way to add more followers to your Facebook profile.

Visual Branding

In a period where there are social media platforms that support only image sharing, you cannot underestimate the power of great visuals. A significant aspect of personal branding on Facebook is your visuals. It should be able to connect your users to your brand. The use of different visuals on each social media platform is a mistake most people make. When building your personal brand, your viewers should be able to identify your brand due to its consistency. It should be the same regardless of the platform.

Having a template can be very helpful. This way you can make sure that the images you share on Facebook are consistent with those on other platforms. A lot of personal brands on social media make use of free tools like Canva to create templates. Sharing a lot of images is another way to get the attention of other users on Facebook. Since the platform depends on your ability to combine images with texts, you should be able to follow it up with a high-quality write-up.

Using Facebook Live

Facebook live offers a means to interact with your followers and meet potential followers. It helps in solidifying the relationship between your personal brand and your fans. It is a streaming video in which you can get personal and creative by providing engaging content.

One of the significant benefits of Facebook Live is how easy you can reach your viewers. All your viewer needs to do is to scroll past your Live video to connect. Once the viewer connects, they have the option of easily posting likes, emojis, and comments. The participation of your viewers is all in real-time.

How to Get the Most of This Feature

The main reason why Facebook users love Facebook Live is the authenticity of the videos. A non-professional feed usually lets your viewers see the real you. A little bit of movement here and there is okay since no one is expecting a video of professional quality. To improve the quality of your Facebook Live videos to an acceptable quality, there are certain aspects you need to improve. The first step is to get a Smartphone which offers good quality video recording. Purchasing a high-end mobile device will provide improvements in both performances as well as better video resolution.

You should also invest a reasonable amount in purchasing a tripod. A tripod offers stability over the use of a selfie stick. Narrating your story while trying to balance a selfie stick can be an arduous task. Tripods are available at various prices with some mini tripods at prices below $25. Nonetheless, it is crucial you find a tripod that is lightweight and portable. Another essential step is to pick a good location when recording a video. The place should have excellent lighting. Direct sunlight behind you is your best bet.

Getting Traffic

To get the most traffic on your Facebook Live Videos, it is essential you create a schedule for your videos. The videos should be on at a time when most of your viewers will be online. It can be when they are on their mobile device or computer. Having a video description is also essential. People should be able to know your guest, your location, what makes the video interesting, and what you will be doing without watching the videos. It is also a more natural way to get new viewers to view your Facebook Live Videos.

Interaction with your audience is a vital aspect of the live video. Getting your audience to reply by commenting and liking your feed can also boost your traffic. During the video, ensure you ask questions. The video becomes more exciting and fun for your users when they are actively participating in what is happening. As I mentioned earlier, you must be authentic. No one is willing to waste time to see a video with a script like a commercial. Produce video content that shows you now and makes it feel like live action.

A sign of appreciation goes a long way when building a personal brand. Remember to do this after saving the video to your feed. It can be a simple "thank you" comment on the video. Remember also to make use of call to action. You can use this to divert traffic to your other social media pages. Just ask your audience to follow you on Twitter, visit your blog, or like your video on Instagram. Facebook Live video is one key tool to help in personal branding since it is free to use.

Using Facebook Insights

Creating content that will interest your audience is a lot easier if you have information on their behavior. Facebook Insights offers the information you need. It provides data which you can use in improving the performance of your personal brand. To gain access to the Facebook Insights on your page, click on the "Insights" at the top of the page. There are lots of tabs which the Insights page offers to Facebook users.

Overview

The first important area to visit is the Overview tab. It offers a page summary and shows metrics for the five most current posts on your page. It also compares other Facebook Pages which are like yours. These are the areas where you can analyze using the overview tab:

- Pages to Watch

- Page summary

- Most Recent Posts

Pages to Watch

The Pages to Watch is one of the great features of Facebook Insights. It is a simple tool which helps in comparing your page to other similar pages. These pages are some of the pages which you need to monitor. It is beneficial in showing how your page is doing against other personal brands in your niche. Clicking on any of the pages will give you a ranking of the posts.

Page Summary

If you want to learn about the key metrics of the Facebook Page, you should visit the Page Summary section. It shows the Reach, Page Likes, and Post Engagement for the past week. There is also a graph to compare changes between the past and the current period. Assessing the performance of your Page with this section is easy. Looking at the Reach and Page Likes can tell you about the growth of the page. The page summary also allows you to export the page metrics as an excel spreadsheet or CSV file.

Most Recent Posts

In this section, you can view relevant information on your five most recent posts. These include the post type, engagement, post caption, reach, targeting, date and time of publishing post. Clicking on the title of a post will give a full breakdown of the performance of a post.

Likes

Knowing the number of likes on a post can get you excited when building your personal brand. The Likes tab takes it a step further. It gives you the opportunity to identify the source of the likes, the growths, and averages. There is a Net Likes section which shows a graph of the likes on your page. It also includes unlike. It will enable you to monitor the 'unlike' trend and 'like' trend to assess the growth of the page. Identifying the source of likes on your page is also another great feature of the Likes tab. It is also a graph that displays the Page likes from Facebook Page suggestions, ads, or direct likes from your page.

Actions on Page

Visiting the Actions on Page section will give you a better understanding of the different actions people take on your page. Clicking on a phone number, website, action button, or "Get Directions" are the actions that Facebook records. In this section, you can view the following:

- People Who Clicked Website

- People Who Clicked Get Directions

- People Who Clicked Phone Number

- People Who Clicked Action Button

- Total Actions on Page

The first four sections are quite similar. Each displays a graph of the number of individuals who performed each action. The Total Actions on Page also displays a graph. In this case, the graph showcases the number of actions that users have performed on your page. The Action Button is a handy button if you have a unique action you want users to take. It can redirect to a sign up on your website or any other action. There are other tabs available on the Insights pages. These include:

- Reach

- Posts

- Page Views

- Videos

- Events

- Messages

- People

Chapter 8:
Creating A Personal Brand on Twitter

Getting Started

Like any social media platform, getting started on twitter involves creating a great profile. There are a few steps to take in building a profile which will have a significant impact on your audience.

SETTING UP YOUR PROFILE

Use Your Real Name

When creating a Twitter handle, using your real name is essential for your personal brand. Since another user may take this name, you can use something very close to this name. It will be difficult for your audience from other platforms to find you on twitter if you use any different name.

Just seeing your handle on a tweet should immediately trigger the memory of your audience. Users should be able to connect the name to your Instagram or Facebook account without any issue. It is also like how popular companies like Twitter and Netflix use handles like @twitter and @netflix. Changing your username or handle is possible but is not always advisable. In addition to the need for consistency, you may also lose your verification badge if you have one.

Use A Real Photo of Yourself

A personal brand requires you to connect with your users. The connection should be on a human level. For this reason, using a picture of you is necessary. Avoid using photos of you with your pets or a group photo. A professional headshot is also great for this purpose. You can opt for a session at a photographer to get the right photo to build your personal brand. Being consistent when uploading your profile photo also helps. Having the same photo across your social media accounts also improves the chances of your audience finding you.

Optimize Your Profile For SEO

SEO optimization is an excellent way to make your account more visible. Including keywords in your bio can help with SEO optimization. These keywords are popular words that a lot of Twitter users search for on the platform. Your bio will also appear in search results when a person inputs your name in an internet search. Therefore, you need to make the most of it. It is also vital you avoid the use of numbers when coming up with a handle or name to avoid looking like a spam account. There are certain descriptions you can add to improve your bio. They include the following:

- The target description – your niche

- An intriguing description – something unique and exciting about you

- A description that makes you human – what you love doing

- Description of your accomplishments

- A professional description

- Link to other social media pages, a blog, or a website

Include A URL

URLs offer an easy way to direct users to another site. Adding a URL to your Twitter profile is an excellent way to generate traffic on your website or blog. In a case where you don't have a website or blog, you can use a URL to redirect users to any other site where you are visible online. It can be Instagram, Facebook, YouTube, etc. Your audience will always want to connect with you outside twitter. URLs offer an easy way to achieve this connection.

What Makes Twitter Valuable for Building A Personal Brand?

There are a lot of benefits to the use of Twitter. It is more than using it to get in contact with your friends and family. Twitter offers users an easy means to make priceless conversations with brands and influencers. Users can also join a conversation on a topic that interests them.

The platform is an excellent choice for publishing, finding, and conversing about news in real time. Also, it also provides the opportunity to share other content. Here are some of the features which make Twitter valuable:

Trends

Following trends is an easy way to keep yourself updated on the latest happenings around the world and in your industry. It also makes it very easy to start conversations with other users and promote you promote your personal brand using hot topics.

Ease of Use

Finding users and influencers within your niche on twitter is very easy. You can tag your favorite influencers in a conversation, mention them in a tweet, or follow them. Getting noticed on twitter is as simple as retweeting posts from other users.

Mobile Friendly

As a social media platform, users always have access to Twitter from their tablets and smartphones. It makes it possible for users to comment, share, and tweet from anywhere and at any time. With a lot of people having access to mobile devices, you can reach more users on the platform.

Specific Audience Targeting

Like other social media platforms like Facebook, Twitter also provides an opportunity for users to target a demographic. You can search for users who are fans of a topic within your niche or users who follow your favorite influencers. Paid and organic messages are also available to reach your target demographic.

STEPS TO TAKE WHEN BUILDING YOUR PERSONAL BRAND ON TWITTER

Building Connections and Influence

When developing a personal brand on social media, you are establishing yourself as an expert in a niche. It means you will be someone that everyone will come to for answers and solutions. These include CEOs, marketers, and other social media users. To achieve your goals, you need to capitalize on Twitter engagements to gain influence and connections. There are various ways to connect with other Twitter users. They include the methods listed below:

Respond to Tweets

Showing love to your followers is a sure way to build their loyalty and trust. As your personal brand grows, it is easy to forget this simple step. Your followers will expect a response from you if they tweet at you. The good idea is to respond to your followers within 24 hours. You can make your task more comfortable by using email notifications and monitoring tools on your account.

Tag, Share and Start Conversations

When building your personal brand on Twitter, you may need to share images, articles, or links which don't belong to you. It is a good idea to tag the author of any article you are posting. It will earn you the respect of both the author and your audience.

Talk! Talk!! Talk!!!

Mentions and replies are the best ways to converse on Twitter. If you are using a mention, you are merely adding the handle of another user to your tweet. It is an option which you use in starting a new conversation. On the other hand, you use replies to continue a conversation which revolves around a tweet from a user.

Use Videos When Possible

Building a personal brand will require you to make smart moves. There is a lot you can share on Twitter using videos. Twitter allows users to upload videos with a maximum duration of 140 seconds. It is easy for most individuals to overlook this simple tool, but there is a lot you can showcase using a video. Making useful videos will improve engagement from your users. The use of videos is more likely to get you retweets and replies than what you get with regular posts.

Use Trends to Your Advantage

One of the best parts of Twitter is the trending section. It shows the topics with the most tweets for each day. Take advantage of this tool. By searching for trending topics, you can pick a topic and relate it to your brand. Create a branding plan which will focus on this topic. New trending topics come up every day, if you don't find any topic that correlates with your brand then wait. There are specific rules you should remember when using trends to your advantage. Here are some of the most important:

- Avoid using too many hashtags

- Do your research on the trending topic

- Make sure you target your market

- Remain neutral on sensitive topics

- Participate in the conversation

Twitter Chats

What better way to connect with other individuals than through chats? Twitter chats help you gain new followers and get informed about the latest updates in your niche. Twitter chats are conversations which usually held on the same day and time. The chats typically focus on a topic or hashtag. It brings people with the same interests together for easy interaction.

The chats usually hold for about an hour during which the host will ask about eight questions which relate to the hashtag or topic in focus. Since it is a community event, members of the community can respond to tweets by using the hashtag which the host selects for the event. By participating in such events, you can interact better using twitter. These chats offer opportunities to collaborate and form relationships with other influencers and brands. In the end, you will gain more followers and establish yourself as an authority.

Use the Follow Button Effectively

An excellent way to remain active on twitter is to follow other users. It also gives you access to new content every day. You can choose to follow up to 5 new users daily. One problem when you follow a lot of users is going through all the new content that appears on your twitter feed. There are two solutions to this problem. The first is to depend on the Twitter algorithm for top contents or create a list.

The Twitter algorithm will decide on what content is best for you to view. The downside to this option is that you will miss some critical content. You may still can catch up on recent posts by scrolling down. Creating a list offers more flexibility. You can create a list that includes the important people on your account. The list should not contain too many users, so it is easy to go through all the tweets. Creating a list for influencers in varying niches is also advisable.

Identifying the right people to follow is also important. You can use the "who to follow" tab to select new followers. This tab suggests new users using your past interactions and recent follows as a basis for the suggestion. You may have the urge to follow a lot of big names on Twitter. The problem with this option is that you may not get their attention. Just consider how many notifications JK Rowling will get daily for a start.

Instead, you should follow other influencers and personal brands with a reasonable number of followers. These influencers are more likely to notice your account. Deciding on the right action to take when a new user follows you is also important. A lot of people recommend that you follow back any new follower. In truth, you must be mindful of who you follow.

As a personal brand, it is best to avoid controversial accounts. A reasonable action is to check the timeline of a new follower over the past few weeks. It will give an idea of the type of content they post. Is it the type of content you want to see? During the process of building your personal brand, having a higher following count than your followers' count is unavoidable. It is one of the easiest ways to drive mutual interaction. A follow is a tool to turn the attention of a user to your account rapidly.

Track Twitter Mentions.

Tracking your mentions on Twitter is an excellent way to improve interaction. It helps in deciding the users you should try to interact with more often. You can take this to the next level by using tracking tools on the internet. These tools include Tweetbeep and Google Alerts. You have the option of inputting a keyword which the tool tracks and alerts you if there is a mention of the keyword. It is effortless to find users who mention you more often with these tools. You can also interact more with these users to solidify your relationship.

Become Better at Tweeting

Building a successful personal brand on Twitter will require you to improve yourself in using twitter. There are a lot of online tools which can be very helpful in improving how you tweet. Finding a tool which makes it easier to find and join conversations is essential. A tool like Mention helps you discover conversations which will be of interest as well as those that involve you. It also allows you to reply with ease directly from the application. Having a scheduling tool is also helpful. You can use this tool in deciding the right time to tweet. Hootsuite and Klout are two useful scheduling tools. They both offer some unique features which attract different users.

Use Pinned Tweets

Twitter allows users to pin a single tweet. The pinned tweet appears at the top of the page. It is possible to change this tweet anytime you desire. There are lots of benefits to using a pinned tweet. It can be a tweet that tells other users why they should follow your page and what to expect, run promotions, and redirect traffic. The tweet also remains at the top for as long as you want. Using a pinned tweet to build your personal brand is very easy. Nonetheless, you should ensure you are pinning the very best. It should be a tweet which will promote retweets and clicks. A link should appear about halfway through if you need to add one.

The rate of retweets for tweets with images is 35% more than those without images. It is according to information from the official Twitter blog. Since a lot of people prefer manual retweets, leave a few characters for them to do it this way. Selecting a tweet to pin is quite easy. All you need to do is to click the three tiny dots that appear close to the 'view tweet activity.' Just select the "Pin" option that appears.

Changing the pinned tweet often will make it look fresh. As a result, it will always remain visible to your viewers. A tweet that makes a follower happy will prompt the user to retweet. Make emotion a weapon in your pinned tweets.

Improve Your Profile

Although setting up your profile is the first thing you do, you still need to tweak it later. You will need to make a few adjustments to ensure that your profile is unique. Trends and the behavior of your audience will also determine areas where you need improvements. Sometimes, the way you set up your profile may bring in the wrong crowd. Once you notice this, make changes before it is too late. Remember to be consistent in the message you upload on your bio.

Remain Active

To be active on twitter, you must tweet regularly. You should try tweeting at least five times a day. It is crucial you tweet about relevant topics. You can start by reading through conversations before coming up with your tweet. It also helps in promoting engagement with your followers, other personal brands, and other users. Posting a unique tweet every day is essential for your personal brand. Include trending hashtags to reach more of your audience. You can make up to two tweets about trending topics each day.

Develop a Blog

Using Twitter is an excellent way to reach your audience with content that is short and straight to the point. It is beneficial when developing your brand voice and creating engagement with your audience. Nonetheless, it can be challenging to establish your expertise on Twitter. That is why a blog is a great option. Using a blog to complement your Twitter account can get you the exposure you need. Your blog is the platform on which you pour out your thoughts. On the other hand, your Twitter account is the platform where you voice out these thoughts.

In most cases, your voice will only show a little of what you are thinking. Sometimes, people want something short. As other times, it is essential they have access to your complete thoughts in order to make sense of the things you say.

Chapter 9:
Creating A Personal Brand on Instagram

Getting Started

If you want to reach a younger audience, Instagram is the right place to start. More than half of the total number of Instagram users fall within the ages of 18 – 29. Since it opens an opportunity to reach a new target audience, it is essential you understand the basics of using Instagram.

Signing Up on Instagram

After installing the Instagram app on your smartphone, you will need to set up an account. You can also choose to register with Facebook if you prefer. Using an email that is the same across your social media accounts is what I recommend. It is essential if you want to receive your social media notifications from all platforms in the same place. The username or personal brand name should also be consistent. It makes it easy for your audience to find you on various platforms.

The Biography

Like how you need to create a bio on Twitter, you also need one on the Instagram account. Following the tips for creating a bio on Twitter will provide the right results on Instagram.

The Profile Picture

Instagram profile pictures sometimes appear very small when users are looking through your account and posts on the news feed. For this reason, you should use a profile picture which offers clarity at a small size. The picture should be a clear picture of you – it's your personal brand. The background of the image should be clean.

Description

By this time, it is possible you have built your personal brand on other social platforms. It doesn't mean you don't need to introduce yourself. You are still looking to attract new members to your audience. The description should include the tagline of your personal brand or the slogan. It should also include an outline of some vital information about who you are.

Add A Link

Like other platforms, Instagram allows users to place a link on their account. It is just a single link. It is the only clickable link that will be available on your account. Any link you are adding should redirect to a relevant page. It can be your website landing page or your product page. Instagram also provides the opportunity for users to update the link and make changes to yield more positive results.

Connect to Other Social Media Accounts

As soon as you set up all the required fields, your final step is to link the Instagram account. It is a link to your accounts on other platforms. Facebook and Twitter are great places to include.

Your Strategy

Building a personal brand on Instagram requires a branding strategy. The strategy should guide you in attracting the right followers to your page. To create a branding strategy, you can consider some of the following aspects:

- Objectives: This is where you outline what you are to achieve with your personal brand. In this case, it is usually many followers.

- Select a niche: Deciding on a niche makes it easy to become an expert that everyone will go-to for solutions. It also becomes easier to provide content that will satisfy the target audience.

- Target audience: Identifying your audience is essential when creating your content plan. It also helps in identifying pages that can help you reach more individuals that will be interested in your page.

- Content planning: Consistency is essential when building a personal brand. Here, you decide on the frequency of posts, the time of each post, and the content of the posts.

- Assessing results: After implementing your strategy, you need to keep track of growth. It includes tracking the number of likes, comments, followers, conversions, and more.

How Instagram Can Be Beneficial To Your Personal Brand

It Is A Platform Built for Smartphones

Users who need to access Instagram need to own a smartphone. With so many individuals who own a smartphone, Instagram provides a wide audience. As more users begin to access the internet using smartphones, they will also be inclined to join Instagram. This increase in users will increase your audience.

It Is Easy to Tailor Content to Meet the Audience

One of the facts about Instagram is that it has a lower percentage of adult users in comparison to a social media platform like Facebook. Due to the smaller population of this audience, it is possible to create content which will appeal to them.

It Improves Visibility

One of the significant problems that most personal brands have with the use of Facebook is the cost of marketing. It means that personal brands with more resources can meet the target audience through paid marketing. On Instagram, if a user follows your account, they will have access to all the contents on your page. There is no way to block your content from their news feed. It means that your brand will be able to gain recognition since your target audience will be able to see everything you post. Although you can grow your brand without having to spend, Instagram also offers a paid advertising option to its users.

It Depends Exclusively on Visual Content

The exclusive contents that users share on Instagram are video and photo posts. It makes it a goldmine for a personal brand. It makes it possible to promote more engagement by the audience. Using photos, you can show your audience your personal brand in action. Behind-the-scene pictures also make it possible for the audience to connect more with your brand. If you have a product or service on offer, you can use photos to display these products in action.

Audience Engagement Is Very High

The stats in Instagram posts are very high. It is possible for users to like more than 4 billion posts in a single day. It is a significant development that your brand can use to its advantage. Considering that most of the users on Facebook now rely on paid adverts to push their posts to the target audience, it means there will be lower engagement rates on the platform. Posts on Instagram have a high chance of being seen by the target audience. It will also make them more likely to post a comment or like the post.

It Is A Great Platform to Develop A Personal Brand

One of the features that make Instagram a great place to build a personal brand is the option of including only a single link. A lot of people may consider it a downside. It is only valid if your main aim was to generate profits. Users who focus on just personal brand building can use this to their advantage. Since your audience understand that you are not trying to redirect them to any other platform, it becomes easier for them to connect with your personal brand. Creating a humanizing personality and providing authentic content promotes trust and solidifies the relationship between your brand and the audience.

Building Your Personal Brand on Instagram

What Makes You Worth Following?

Are you providing value? Are you entertaining? Or do you offer high-quality content? These are essential questions to ask yourself to determine if you are worth following by other users. Unless you offer one of these, no user will waste their time following your page.

Choose Your Style and Theme

Any new visitor to your page will be able to see your Instagram feed. The Instagram feed contains your posts in a grid format. How this feed will appear to a visitor depends on the style you choose to follow. The style of your account is the mood or tone of the page. It can be colorful, minimalist, dark, vintage, or natural. In simpler terms, it determines the colors that make your color palette.

As a brand influencer, you need to choose a color that defines you. Some brands may stick to a single color for all their posts. Others may decide on a color which will appear once in a row. What is important is that you pick 3 to 5 colors which will dominate your Instagram feed. Experimentation can help in identifying these colors. The background colors are also essential.

Having a single filter which you use frequently can also help in shaping the style of your page. The theme of your posts is the mainstay of your account. When building a personal brand, you must create cohesion between your posts. There should be a few similar topics about which you post.

If you decide that you will build your brand around fitness, then you shouldn't be making posts relating to gaming. Instead, you can make posts that relate to proper exercise techniques. You can also make posts about healthy eating habits. Your posts should be self-explanatory and appealing to make your prospective followers love it at first glance. For this reason, limiting your posts to about three topics is important.

Your Instagram feed is the first thing any potential follower will see about your page. Having a style and a theme will make this feed more attractive.

What Hashtags to Use

If you learn how to use Hashtags effectively, you can build up a large following in a short time. Hashtags serve as one of the most efficient ways to push your content to a lot of people Instagram users.

As useful as this tool is, it is crucial you don't overuse it. Using more than 10 Hashtags on a single picture is overkill. You can limit the number of hashtags to a maximum of 6 per post. Choosing your hashtags wisely is important. You can start by scrolling through the pages of influencer accounts within your niche. It will give you an idea of trending hashtags to use.

If you are building your personal brand in the gaming industry, there are certain popular trends at each period. Trends in the gaming industry can revolve around a new game release or gaming competitions like ESports. There are two options when it comes to selecting a hashtag. These include the following:

Creating your hashtag is another beneficial option. In this case, you can combine words to have more impact. It is also an opportunity for your audience to make use of your hashtag to get a feature on your page. Here are a few areas that can help in deciding the right words:

- Category – this can be either your niche or industry

- Brands – improve your chances of getting a feature by including names of some famous brands within your niche

- Descriptive – what is the story behind the photo?

- Location – your current position

Using two words in creating a hashtag enhances the impact. Learn to include words which your audience use in describing your brand.

Instagram Stories

Instagram Stories offers users a lot of features which promote engagement between you and your followers. Below are some of the tools which are available.

Questions

It is a feature which allows your followers to ask you questions on your Instagram Stories. You can also choose to give a public reply to each question in another story.

Polls

This feature is like the Questions feature. In this case, you are asking your users a question so you can get honest feedback. It is also a positive way to empower your audience.

Instagram Stories Takeovers

If you want to attract new followers to your Instagram page, then Instagram Takeovers is a feature you must be willing to use. By networking with influencers or brands within your niche on Instagram, you can let an influencer or brand take over your account for a day.

If you are lucky to take over the account of an influencer with a large following, then you can gain new followers by sharing high-quality content on their page.

Swipe Up Links

It is a feature which allows Instagram users to attach links to a video or picture before sharing it on their Instagram stories. A significant benefit of this feature is the opportunity to move your followers from Instagram to any platform of your choice. The user only needs to swipe up on the picture or video. There are other features which promote interaction on Instagram Stories. It is essential you prepare to reply to a lot of Direct Messages (DMs) when using Instagram Stories. It is often as a result of the message bars which are included on Instagram stories which don't have links.

Create Connections – And Remove the Chaff

Another easy way to get your profile to your target audience is by following other users. You can also use this method to stay informed. Is there a brand or company you admire? Then follow their page to get information on events, promotions, and company updates. Some businesses also use their social media pages to share interviews which usually don't appear on their webpage. In your bid to create connections, you may end up following the wrong accounts. These are accounts that paint you in a bad light. Quickly unfollow such accounts to prevent any issues. It is easy to become guilty by association when you follow accounts that are quite controversial.

Redirect Followers to Your Blog or Website

Redirecting your followers to your other pages is another critical way to develop your brand. It is possible on Instagram by merely adding a link. The only downside of this feature is that you only have room for a single link on your bio.

Although this is a considerable downside, you must make the most of it. If you run a blog or a website, it is more beneficial to use the link to redirect people to these sites. It increases your chances of getting customers to pay for your services. During the initial stages, you can get more people to click on the link by doing a giveaway or promotion. The link should redirect users to the landing page of the website or blog. Promotions and giveaways may increase traffic, but you shouldn't depend on them for too long. People are more likely to get a full picture of the website if the link redirects to the homepage. Offering high-quality content on the site will make it more attractive to visitors.

Use Geotagging

When building a personal brand on Instagram, you shouldn't underestimate the value of geotagging. The term geotagging implies adding location-specific information like latitude, longitudes, altitudes, etc., to your media. On Instagram, the geotag feature makes it possible to share your content with both your followers and users who don't follow your page. It is also straightforward to use.

If you don't find a geotag that meets your requirements, you can create one through the Facebook "Create a Location" setting. It is accessible through your Facebook account. After submission, you can search for the geotag on Instagram to use it. The "Location" stickers on the Instagram stories also has the same effect. Since your audience can see your location, it becomes easier to get them to reach out. You can end up having lunch with some of your fans around your location to improve your personal brand.

Improve Photos with Apps

Instagram has become quite popular as a photo and video sharing app. What better way to improve your visibility by uploading high-quality photos? If you can use the various tools like geotags and hashtags without providing great photos, you won't be able to grow as a personal brand. The problem with a lot of Instagram users is that they upload photos with poor quality. Using filters to try and improve the photos only make it worse. Cliché filters are quite standard on Instagram. Instead, why not opt for a photo editing app to improve the quality of your posts?

You Need to Go Personal

There is a critical difference between a personal brand and a business. It lies in how they handle situations. A business is expected to handle situations professionally. As a personal brand – be personal! Sharing a few details about your personal life is okay. A lot of your followers will be happy to see such posts. In most cases, what you post about really doesn't matter – a picture of your cat, you and your partner, a vacation, etc. Your audience wants to know that you are human. Let people see the face behind the brand. Simple steps like this differentiate your personal brand from other regular business pages.

Drop A Reply

There is a reason why this tip is on this list. When building a personal brand, interacting with your audience is very important. In truth, applying this tip may become difficult as your audience expands. Nonetheless, it is an important rule to follow while growing your personal brand. Posting a "thank you" comment can go a long way in developing your brand. The only exception is if it's a troll. For posts which get about 50 comments or less, you should be able to reply to each comment. Although it is quite simple, the primary key to success on Instagram is by interacting with your audience.

Like Photos

Since you are trying to get more people to see your page, then you can attract them by liking their pages. The easiest way to do this is to go to your explore tab and like the posts that appear. If you find a post you don't like, click on the three tiny dots and select the "See fewer posts like this" option.

Depending on how much people you want to attract, you can set your target to 200 posts a day. Repeat this process over a period to get more people to see your page. To improve the efficiency of this process, like posts from your target audience or those within your niche. You can do this by searching for trending hashtags within your niche and liking the posts that appear. Another easy way to select posts to like is to explore your favorite locations and like posts from these places.

Chapter 10:
How to Capitalize on Personal Branding

After building a successful personal brand, the next step is to look for opportunities to make money from the brand. It is common for most personal brands to have a product which they offer to their followers at a price. There are other options available to make money from the personal brand. I will be mentioning some of the options available.

WHAT ACTIVITIES CAN EARN MONEY

Selling Digital Products

Digital products have become very popular with the rise of social media. Some of the unique features of digital products are that unlike the physical products, there is no need for an inventory, and it requires little money capital. The problem of having an excess stock doesn't affect digital products. Creating numerous copies of these digital files is possible. The number of digital products you can sell is also not limited. Online storage systems usually create copies of your digital products automatically to prevent such limitations. Digital products you can sell include mp4 videos, mp3 files, and eBooks.

Creating An eBook

As an expert in a niche, people will look forward to learning from you. What better way to reach out to your audience than through an eBook? These eBooks are informational guides which can be steps or how to guides. Examples include 7 Steps to Becoming A Successful Investor or How to Become A Forex Trader.

Offering Coaching and Consultation Services

Since you have been able to establish yourself as an expert in a specific niche, you can offer coaching and consultation services within this niche. A successful personal brand provides the credibility you need to attract prospects. It is also important you understand the difference between a coaching service and a consultation service.

A coaching service will help in identifying the weaknesses and strengths of a client and offering methods to develop these areas. On the other hand, the consultation service identifies an issue that a business is battling and provides a solution to address this issue. Providing a consultation service to a prospect is an excellent way to identify the challenges they currently face. It also helps in deciding issues which may be difficult to handle. You can then charge for your services appropriately.

Implementing Google AdSense Ads

Google AdSense ads provide an easy way for you to earn passive income. It allows site owners to display targeted ads on their platform.

Getting the ads on your page is also free. All you need to do is apply which will be reviewed. If your application is successful, you will receive an email within a week. There are policies you need to follow to remain a part of the program. If you are consistent in the type of content you post, you should have no problem. There are policies which you must strictly follow to remain part of the program. Part of the policies relates to the type of content on your site.

The ads that appear on your site is chosen on the other end. You don't have the option of selecting the advertisements. It is optimized to suit your audience and the type of content on your site. Although you must avoid coercing visitors to click on the ads, you make money depending on the number of users that click on these ads. Using Google Analytics is also helpful in checking the performance of the ads on your page.

Developing an Online Course

Offering an online course is an easy way to make money from your personal brand. Your audience will have an interest in the things you have to offer. A lot of users prefer to follow steps which are specific while also delivering results within a given timeframe. When creating your course, you can choose to go down the path of an expert or be a curious novice. As an expert, you are sharing the knowledge you already have. As a curious novice, you are teaching your audience a skill as you learn it.

For your first online course, you can choose to start small. Regardless, it is essential you create a course outline to decide how you will transition between topics. Once you have an outline, develop the content. Selecting a topic which you are passionate about is an easy way to boost engagement. The topic for your online course can relate to your talents, life experiences, or skills. The topic you pick should also be like what a lot of people are talking about, but the content should be unique.

Providing a high-quality learning outcome is also essential. None of your followers will be willing to pay for a course without a clear understanding of what they will gain at the end. Your learning outcome will show your followers the skills, knowledge, and changes they will be able to make at the end of the course. The course content should be well progressively structured into themes and modules. You also need to decide what method will be the best for content delivery. Having the right balance of practical, audio, and visual means will have the most impact.

Affiliate Marketing

A successful personal brand is usually one with many followers. Your ability to influence your followers is another sign of success. What better way to use this influence on your advantage than through affiliate marketing? Affiliate marketing is an excellent way to gain additional revenue on your social media platforms. To achieve this goal, you will need to become a part of an affiliate marketing network.

There are a few of these networks that rank among the best. These include:

- eBay

- Clickbank

- ShareASale

Your job on this network is simple; you help others promote a service or product. The products you choose to promote should be those that have a very close relation to the niche of your personal brand. It is an excellent step to take to avoid looking like spam.

To be successful in affiliate marketing, you need to be patient. You should also understand that you can only take full advantage of your high-quality content if the affiliate product links you provide are also of high quality. Using a redirect link is also recommended since it appears neater. Since you are on a social platform, why not get social? There are lots of affiliate marketers online and creating a network will be a great benefit. Cooperating with other marketers will offer more benefits than considering them as your competition.

Becoming A Public Speaker

There are lots of benefits you can gain from public speaking. For anyone just building a personal brand, public speaking can help to establish you as an expert in your niche. By becoming an authority within your niche, you can grow your fan base quickly.

Once people consider you as an authority, it becomes easier to make money from public speaking. Everyone wants a moment of your time to pick your brain. In addition to getting paid, you can leverage such public speaking opportunities to gain more followers, advertise your services or products, and increase traffic to your social media pages.

Hosting Webinars

A webinar is an online form of a seminar. In simpler terms, it is a seminar which you conduct over the internet. One of the main benefits of webinars is the reduction in costs since you are not renting a location. Webinars can be very profitable if you use it correctly. To make it work, you need many people who are willing to tune in to the webinar. Therefore, it is excellent for anyone who runs a personal brand.

The content of the webinar or the presentation itself is usually free. It is how you attract more people to the brand. To make money from the webinar, you should offer a paid product at the end of the program. If the information you offer during the webinar is of high quality and there has been adequate promotion to attract people, you can sell a lot of your products. A user will only be willing to pay for your information if they can learn a lot from the free webinar. You should consider the webinar as a free trial of your product.

It is also important you understand human nature when hosting a webinar. It is common to notice a drop in your attendees after about 45 minutes into the webinar. It is why it is crucial that you pitch the product after about 30 minutes into the webinar. Infographics and visuals also aid your pitch to a high degree.

Capitalizing on Crowdfunding

Diving into new projects is an excellent way to make things go better for your brand. Sometimes, the main limitation is the lack of funds. Your brand can help in achieving the funds you require. If you have an exciting idea to share, you can reach out to crowdfunding networks and your audience to raise funds. The funds may be necessary to cover the production costs or purchase equipment of a higher quality.

Providing a sneak preview to your audience is an easy way to get people interested in the project. It means you need to create time to make a great video. The video should explain what the project is about and showcase a little bit of the project. Kickstarter and Indiegogo are popular crowdfunding websites you can visit. These are sites which are very popular among YouTube users. Fan Funding streams is another option which is available to raise donations from your audience. All through the development of your brand, you have depended on your high-quality content. If the audience loves your content, it is easier to get them to support your page.

Selling A License to Your Content

One of the popular methods of gaining recognition on social platforms like YouTube is by sharing a video that goes viral. For any video to go viral, there must be a reasonable amount of appeal. It is what you leverage for an additional income.

Since the viral video is your creation, you own the rights to the use of the videos. Various content creators from online news websites, TV news outlets, Morning shows, and more can reach out. Everyone will be rushing to gain the rights to this video. There are also other online marketplaces which make it easy for both you as the creator and any potential buyer. By listing the content on the marketplace, it is easier for the buyer to find the content they need. An example of such a marketplace is Junken Media.

Becoming A Member of the YouTube Partner Program

As a personal brand, building a YouTube channel with a large following will provide opportunities to make money. The YouTube Partner Program is the chance to make money through adverts. This program is usually more beneficial to channels that already generate a lot of views and clicks. As a successful personal brand channel, it means you can profit from this program. There are a few steps you need to take to become a part of the program. I will be discussing these steps below.

Signing Up

The first step is to sign up for the YouTube Partner Program. Channels that have generated a minimum of 10,000-lifetime views of YouTube are eligible to join the program. There is also an age restriction on the use of the YouTube payment system. The payment system is only available to individuals who are 18 or older. In a case where you are below this age, ask someone who meets the age requirements to open a family account. The Program is available in only some countries, so you need to check if you live in a country on the list.

Activate Monetization and Accept the Terms of The Program

On your YouTube account, go to the channels tab and open the Status features. Locate the "Monetization" tab and select the "Enable" option. You will also need to read the terms of the YouTube Partner Program. It is important you understand these terms before you agree and click on the "accept" option. Some of the terms include providing original content on your page. It is also essential you go over the YouTube community guidelines to ensure you are in good standing.

Choose Your Monetizing Options and Approve Your Enrolment

There are three options available when monetizing. These include Videos Contain a Product Placement, Overlay In-Video Ads, and TrueView In-Stream Ads. The Videos Contain a Product Placement implies that an ad or short commercial will play before your video starts playing. It is also the same in the TrueView In-Stream Ads.

The Overlay In-Video Ads will add a banner which will take space on the video window while it plays. The ads will appear automatically on your page regardless of the option. You can choose one option or decide to select the three options. The opportunity to adjust the types of ads will be available in the future. The next step is to select the "Monetize My Videos" to approve your enrolment into the YouTube Partner Program.

Wait for A Reply

If you follow the YouTube community guidelines, you should receive approval. It is usually within a short time. Once your application is confirmed, there will be a "Partner Verified" status on your YouTube channel. The adverts you select during your sign-up process will immediately start to appear on the channel. It implies that you immediately begin earning from the program.

It is also possible to not receive approval. It means that the content on your channel has been assessed doesn't appear to be authentic. Violence, sexually explicit content, and hate speech in your videos may also affect your chances. You can choose to remove these videos and then apply for the program later.

Chapter 11:
Strategies for Success in Personal Branding

Having Good Role Models

Selecting a role model often has a way of shaping the life of an individual. A good role model is a person who has a decent character with the right morals. A role model should also be at the top in their field.

Being realistic in your expectations is also important when deciding on a role model. You should expect them to have a few flaws. Nonetheless, these weaknesses should not limit their ability to inspire others. By learning from a role model, it is possible to develop strength from weaknesses. They teach us that your shortcomings should not be a hindrance to our goals.

Getting Motivation from Role Models

When working towards a goal, it is common to start with enthusiasm and high spirits. As humans, difficulties and challenges can quell any excitement you had about a goal. A good role model will serve as a source of motivation in achieving your goals. They will make it possible for you to rise above any challenge or difficulty. It is because they will have a lot of experience since they have faced most of the challenges at different points in their life.

FINDING THE RIGHT ROLE MODELS

Family

In life, the first people we consider to be our role models are our parents and grandparents. Since they are the people, we interact with more during our early years, it is easier to learn their principles and values. The struggles and stories of our parents can serve as a learning opportunity. It is an easy way to identify the path they took that led to failures and those that led to success. The lessons available to serve as a guide is quite extensive.

Learning from History

Historical records are an excellent place to find individuals that can serve as excellent role models. It is also possible to find individuals from different areas of life. It doesn't matter if your interest is in science, showbiz, personal brand, politics, and others. So many vital people fall into these various categories. Anyone from the list can quickly illuminate your life and direct you to the right path.

Biographies

People who make an impact are always the center of focus. Therefore, there are usually biographies about them. Going through the biography of an individual will give you a clear picture of the steps they took to become successful. Some high achievers required a lot of hard work and determination to reach success. Others may have been lucky along the way. The biography of an individual will show the important aspects you can add to your routine.

Have Multiple Role Models

Having multiple role models can help in developing your life at its various stages. Multiple role models also offer a lot of good qualities which you can identify and combine to improve your life. Remember, one role model cannot have all the qualities that will be beneficial to you.

Select the Right Mentors

A lot of times, personal brand owners do not look for the right mentor early enough. They Give reason like, 'why would I need a mentor?' 'Who is capable of mentoring me?' There is nothing bad in paying for mentors. It can be through private arrange a coach or a personal brand mentor. You should be aware that most states have a mentoring program that is run by the government. These programs are often subsidized to give the small-scale personal brand the opportunity to partake. I will provide them with the privilege to access the expertise and advice from personal brand owners that are more experienced.

If you don't have the means to pay for mentoring, you can arrange for an unpaid mentor who would be pleased to spend some time with you every few months. You should not take much of their time since they are offering you free service. Therefore, make sure you give the relationship the respect it deserves, keep the duration of your meeting with them as short as possible, and appreciate them warmly at the end of each session.

Anybody that volunteers to mentor you without collecting a dime is helping you in a significant way. So, it is important to consider anything you can do to reciprocate the kind gesture. You will be amazed at the generosity of some influential people when you asked them for advice. The problem is the only few people have the nerve to ask questions.

Block Out Negativity

It is not uncommon for your friend, family, and even your schoolmates to have a varying opinion about your new personal brand. They will always have one or two things to say about what you are doing. People that do not own a personal brand often fall into these two categories:

- The ones that give you encouragement to carry on with anything you are doing. Regardless of what you are involved in, they will always cheer you up to continue. Those categories of people are just doing the polite thing. "You are doing great," "oh, what a great idea you have got,"

- The second category of people are the ones that discourage you from taking a risk. These are the kind of people who always think about the negative side of the situation. Such people will always say – "Do you have what it takes to get on twitter- what you do something wrong? That's going to affect your brand negatively", "Do you think it is advisable to change the color of your brand to Red? Please don't stop the customers because red means stop."

The Advice here is to block out people that always discourage you from forging ahead with your plans. Do not take the advice of the naysayers and never buy into everything the first category of people is saying either. All you need to do is get yourself a group of personal brand owners that agree with your line of thought and move with people who have the perfect understanding of what you are going through.

It is essential you hang out with people with a good vision for their lives and personal brand. You should think about the attitude of people you are moving it whether it is good for your mindset.

Yes, there is a likelihood of negative publicity. You will attract more negative attention if you misrepresent yourself, get involved in some controversial issue, r you misinterpret someone in an article. You should know the more you put yourself out there, the higher the chances of this happening. It is one of the risks associated with content creation and social media marketing, but the issue with personal marketing is that there is no simple way to reduce it.

Once you are stigmatized or you have a bad reputation, it can be difficult to redeem your image, the stigma could follow you for the rest of your life. A bad reputation can result from a google search bringing up the incident, which could affect the future.

Although there are some potential drawbacks of personal branding, it is still an excellent strategy for personal brand owners and job seekers. It is indispensable in this modern world. You can meticulously work to maximize the benefits if you are aware of the risks involved. You can strategically mitigate the risk while you maximize the gains. Just like any other career venture, it is essential you reexamine your effort along the way, estimating your return on investment. You can always withdraw if it feels like the venture is no longer worth it.

Measuring Analytics Via Social Media

The first thing you need to understand about social media is how it can help you estimate the power and reach of your customer's through social media platforms. That is, these metrics help to gauge the performance of the social media channel. Then, you can make use of the information to analyze your content to optimize a strategy to develop your personal brand. Click-through rate is an excellent example of social media analytic metric. The click-through rate is the percentage of people clicking your link via social media updates to your actual website.

It looks simple enough, but it is not so, it can be quite complicated. This is because analytics involves lots of data. The information is processed and analyzed to develop a social media strategy that is in line with your target. The analysis is based on the combination of expertise and experience in this area. You can get insight into an area like audience growth, content arrangement, and customer service through social media services. Are you willing to attract new customer through your social media? Are you posting something that will engage the customers? How fast does your customer service team attend to customers' need through social media? Are you getting a positive response from your customers? You will get an answer to these questions and many other related questions from social media analytics.

Leveraging the Numbers to Increase Your Market Presence

It may be a bit confusing here; analytics is entirely different from simple engagement through social media. It is straightforward to consider the number of inquiries you received and the way you responded to them all. That is an engagement. When it comes to analytics, you can find out where these inquiries came from, how you can attend to them quickly, their behavior when during social media engagement. It is what you need to tailor your message according to the requirements or needs of your audience.

Single number or analytics will not do the trick. The more the data available, the better when it comes to analytics. This comprises the data from customers as well as competitors. The social media content topics are based on the data available from the two sources.

Also, it also determines whether the content will be in video format, text or graphs. The data may be overwhelmingly numerous, but every bit of what is gathered is significant when it comes to the development of effective social media strategy. You may not have a complete picture of what is required when you rely on limited data.

How Does Analytics Help?

As mentioned earlier, social media is a great tool and can have a remarkable impact on your bottom line if done correctly. There are three significant areas where social media can boost your personal brand' growth.

Customer Service

According to research, about 67% of the customers have meet a brand via social media platform and have asked customer service-related questions through this platform. You can expand your reach by sharing the questions and answers via a social media platform.

Build Your Brand

The ability of social media to build your brand cannot be overestimated. Thousands of customers can share imaging promoting your brand through the social media platform. Social media platform is a fantastic place to share positive pictures of your products as well as your brand personality.

Make A Sale

The primary goal of any campaign is to convert prospects into buyers. Social media is very powerful in this regard. It has been discovered from the latest research in from Sprout social media that 49% of customers purchase can be prompted when you answer questions that are related to customers on social media.

Data-Driven Strategy

It is quite easy to know if your investment in content creation was worth it when you leverage the data collated through social media analytics. It is a continuous process that should not stop with the first social media post. It is essential to analyze data continually to ensure that you are benefiting from your investment. You should not forget that the amount of data that is gathered and analyzed is essential as it ensures that your social media tactic is meeting your needs as far as marketing is concerned.

Dealing with Growth

Growth is constant and inevitable. It affects trends, society, priorities, and technology. As a personal brand, you must be ready to deal with this growth when it comes. In your personal brand, the changes are usually positive in the form of growth. Adjusting to these changes will not require a noticeable revamp of your process. All it needs is a little tweak in certain areas which will account for growth in your target audience. In order to remain relevant as a brand, you need to meet the needs of your target audience consistently. It includes both the new members of the audience and those who have been members for a long time. You can start by updating contents or re-imagining some of your old ideas.

What Makes Growth Difficult for A Personal Brand?

There are various reasons why you need to be subtle when making changes to your personal brand strategy. It all has to do with your target audience. As humans, there are some specific reasons why change is difficult. It includes the following:

It Causes Stress on The Brain

Humans depend on habits to live. It is a more efficient and effective method to complete the activities of a day. If a change is to come, what is the indication that it will be a positive change? Will it be an improvement to current habits?

Using an Old Brain Map on A New Idea

A sudden change can be very hard on an individual if they don't get time to adjust for the change properly. It is the same way a great football player will find it difficult to perform at the top level the first time playing in snowy conditions.

The Unfamiliar

Change is something that is unfamiliar to your audience. It is the same way they will move to another brand if you try to feed them content that doesn't align with their interests.

How Will You Adjust Your Brand for Growth?

The growth of your audience to include individuals from different de-mographics will often result in the need for change. To effectively adapt your content to meet the growing audience there are two steps to take. Understanding the audience better: when creating your con-tent, you need to learn the different approaches through which you can reach different audience groups. To make your content effective, you need to tweak the content to meet each audience group.

Establish objectives: clearly stating the objectives of your content will help you assess its effectiveness. It will involve assessing the feed-back, comments, likes, and general reactions. Understanding the per-formance of each content will make it possible to improve the subse-quent contents to meet the demands of the audience.

Why Do Some Personal Brands Fail?

Personal branding is a difficult task which takes time. The process can be prolonged which is why a lot of people lose focus while others may give up. The inability of individuals to handle negative feedback will also affect the personal brand. There are a few areas where per-sonal brands make mistakes. Assessing these areas can help you im-prove your personal brand. Here are some things that may hurt your personal brand building:

Not Connecting with Other Influencers

When building a personal brand, you are likely going to be in a niche where other individuals are building their brand. These individuals may have been in the process for a longer time.

By listing these brands and monitoring them, you will be able to identify areas where you can get an idea to improve your brand building. Proper research will help in determining the aspects that these other brands have covered. You can also locate other personal brands that will be willing to become partners. Taking the advice of others who have more experience helps to avoid wasting resources.

Offering Low-Quality Content

So, you finally have a large audience that listens to you. Is it the right time to lower the quality of your content? Reading wide and staying updated on the new happenings in your niche is important. Ensure your writing remains of high-quality.

Disregarding Your Followers

As soon as you have enough followers, you need to pay attention to them. You want your audience to listen to you. In the same way, they also want you to listen to them. Listen to feedback from your audience regarding the content you post. Why do they like it? Why do they dislike it? You can also learn more about your personal brand through a quick online search.

Branding Yourself Wrong

Building a personal brand that doesn't attract an audience is possible if you fail to perform proper research. Your personal brand should be authentic. It is easy to develop your brand if you are natural.

Failure to Implement A Plan for The Long Term

Where is your brand heading? This is a question which positions a brand for the long-term. A simple example is if you decide to offer beginner tutorials on how to write codes. As your audience follows you for a long time, they will cover all the beginner tutorials and need to advance. Will you move on to the advanced levels? Creating a plan that includes this long-term strategy will make it possible to follow a logical progression.

Inconsistency

In personal branding, consistency is a crucial factor. Your users can only trust you if you are consistent with your belief. If your belief changes at the slightest indication of trouble, no one will believe the content you deliver. Your followers want content that offers thoughts that follow their interests. It is a fundamental belief which they do not like to change.

Chapter 12:
Become the Next Million Dollar Brand

As I discussed in this book, understanding the meaning of a brand is the first step towards your success in personal branding. It is also important you know how to differentiate your brand from your business. The growth of social media within the last decade has made it a powerful tool in building your personal brand. There are different social media platforms available and learning to use them is quite easy. They offer access to an audience which is normally impossible to reach.

Taking your first steps and learning the strategies you can implement in building a brand is necessary. Gaining a better understanding of these strategies will help you reposition your brand for success. Your target audience is the foundation of a brand. How will you connect to the audience? Do you understand the need for conversion tools? How do you intend to find opportunities to expand your brand audience?

There are four main social media platforms which I have mentioned in this book. What platform are you familiar with? Have you been able to establish any connections with influencers on any of these platforms? Is there something you are doing wrong? Did you incorporate the long-term money-making plan into your personal branding strategy? If not, what was your goal for creating a personal brand? There are certain crucial personal branding tips which this book promotes. They include the following:

Being an Expert

If you are not an expert in any niche, then it will be difficult to create a personal brand. By taking a quick look at some of the best personal brands and influencers, you will notice that they focus on a niche.

If you want to sell fitness products, you should have both the knowledge and the body of a fitness expert. If you're going to build your brand around daredevil stunts, you should be able to perform these stunts. Another way to build a brand is to focus it around a niche where you have worked. If you were an automobile salesman, you could develop a brand around car parts.

Authenticity

Authenticity in personal branding implies that you need to be yourself. What makes you unique as an individual? You may enjoy speaking in rhymes or cross-dressing. These are quirks which you can use to your advantage. To build a successful personal brand, you must accept your quirks. Being authentic is the only way to stand out in any niche you decide to focus on.

Consistency

All successful personal brands are consistent. It doesn't imply being active on social media daily. It has to do with the appearance of your brand and your content. Are you able to produce content that looks the same? Your followers will lose interest if you move from make-up content to automobile content. They are following you because you offer content that interests them.

Value

Offering value means there is something useful which you offer your audience. It is not all about making money to you. It is more of providing something that will develop your audience. If you are building a personal brand around the laptops, you will want to provide instructional videos. These can be how-to videos on cleaning a laptop fan, changing the hard drive, and so on. Since you have been providing free helpful information, your audience is more likely to buy a product you are selling when it is available.

Networking

Meeting new people is an essential aspect of personal brand building. It involves interactions with followers, influencers, and other users. When creating a network, you can expand to other niches. It is an excellent way to develop relationships which may be helpful in the future. You should also attend conferences and events regularly. This is an excellent form of socialization with other users.

Develop Yourself as A Creator

Creating your content is a good way to develop your personal brand. You should also come up with new ideas. This includes a new product, service, video, etc. You must keep producing new content to get noticed.

My Final Words to You

There are many benefits you can gain from building a personal brand. One of the most important benefits is the growth it offers your business. If you have read this book, I believe you have a goal you are striving to achieve. A lot of information is contained within this book to steer you in the right direction when creating your personal brand. The book focuses on social media as your major tool for personal branding. Social media offers a lot of benefits to a personal brand— it is cheaper, offers a larger audience, better targeting options, and many more.

Nonetheless, this tool will go to waste if you are not willing to put in the work. I'm not telling you it will be easy – good things don't come easy. Read this quote from Jeff Bezos.

"A brand for a company is like a reputation for a person. You earn reputation by trying to do hard things well." –Jeff Bezos, Amazon Founder, and CEO

What I want you to know is that you won't be able to promote the unique services you have to offer if you keep procrastinating. Put yourself out there; take a risk. The power to make a difference is in your hands. I urge you to take that step.

If you find this book helpful in anyway a review to support my endeavors is much appreciated.

Social Media Marketing Plan How To

Gary Murphy